Marriage Magic!

Find It, Keep It, and Make It Last

Karen Sherman, Ph.D.

and Dale Klein, M.A.

Kardal Publishing, New York

ISBN: 978-09796808-0-9 (Paperback)

Library of Congress Control Number: 2007904500

This book is printed on acid free paper.

Printed in the United States of America

LaVergne, TN

DEDICATION

Karen and Dale would like to dedicate this book to their spouses, Rich and Steve. They have been our inspiration for keeping the magic going.

Our appreciation to the support from Lindsay and Courtney and to the loves of their lives. And special thanks to Cliff Carle for all of his professional input.

PREFACE

Being involved in a meaningful relationship is one of the most important concerns to most people. As a psychologist, I have often said that a good deal of my practice would not exist if people could find the "right" person. And for a good many of us, we do, indeed find the person that we *believe* will be the answer to our dreams — someone who will be our friend, lover, and partner for life. I know I did. I can remember self-righteously boasting to friends about the terrific marriage I had. And then I gradually realized that the marriage I thought I had was more a fantasy I created. The reality was that I was not happy, did not feel understood or cared about, and certainly the spark was not there. We were certainly busy - each of us with vital careers, not to mention our two children. Was divorce a consideration? Well, maybe — but that didn't quite seem to be the answer. I let my husband know how unhappy I was — it was not easy nor was the period that followed.

As a therapist, I have always felt strongly that I should not offer assistance to others that I would not do myself. My husband and I decided to try to make things work. What was especially poignant for me was the fact that I always stress to others the need for them to take responsibility. In other words, if you want something to change, you have to be the one to make the change. Though, most of us would easily agree with that statement in *concept*, what most of us find easier to do in *action* is to blame other people and expect them to change. But I also know that when one person in a relationship changes, it is very likely that the other person will change in response to the difference.

I began the process. I set out to look at my responsibility in the relationship - what did I do or not do that helped or hurt our partnership. What could I change? I also always kept in mind that change is not a quick process but a gradual one made up of small steps.

After all, the state we were in was not one that happened overnight and would take time to undo. Slowly and gradually, I acted differently and I experienced my husband doing the same. As he started responding, I started to see some positive things that gave me more incentive to try even more, to be more hopeful. We were on our way.

After a relatively short period of time, we started to get a marriage that we both felt good about. Not one that is perfect - because there is no such thing. But it is a partnership that provides us with understanding, satisfaction, and joy. It is one that we are each committed to in ways that are authentic and in touch with what is really going on.

The difficulties of my marriage had been shared with Dale. She is my sister. And as things started to pick up, the benefits were shared, too. Her marriage had not gone through the struggles that mine had. She had taken great strides not to repeat the mistakes made by our parents who had a very negative, conflict-ridden, and abusive relationship.

While my professional efforts were in marital therapy, hers were in communication skills. As we talked, we realized how the seemingly different paths we took really had a lot in common (though the book is truly a collaboration of our two fields of expertise, the references to similar couples have been drawn from Karen's practice. Therefore, when the first person, I, is being used, assume that Karen is speaking).

The more we discussed, the more we realized that the best word to encompass a healthy relationship is one that is "mindful." Among many things, being mindful includes an awareness of your feelings, paying

their favorite table in the corner holding hands. While looking into each

other's eyes, they share their thoughts and exchange stories of the day.

When they get home that evening they curl up in each other's arms in

bed and enjoy laughter, caressing and their special intimacy before

drifting off to sleep.

(Present day....)

Bob and Sue have been married for fifteen years and we once again

meet up with them during the week. Bob calls Sue at her job.

BOB: Hey, Sue, I just have a minute but I wanted to call and see if you

    could pick up the dry cleaning on your way home from work.

SUE: Oh, no way tonight. I've had a lousy day and the last thing I feel

    like is making a stop before getting home.

BOB: Jeez. Oh, all right, I'll do it. So whadaya want to do tonight?

SUE: I don't know. Let's talk about it later. Gotta go, bye.

When Sue arrives home that night, Bob is in his usual couch position,

watching sports on TV and doesn't acknowledge her arrival until she

stands directly in front of him. They exchange a few quick words about dinner and decide on heating up leftovers. Once they are at the table with their two children, they make a few attempts to catch up on the day's events but the phone rings twice and their children each have school projects they need to discuss, and then dinner's over. Bob and Sue meet up again around 11:00 in their bedroom and fall into bed, exhausted. Sue turns to Bob to kiss him, but he's already fast asleep. At first Sue finds herself relieved that she doesn't have to "perform" tonight, then suddenly, she becomes sad. She rolls over, and wonders to herself, *where did things go wrong?* Sad as it might be, most marriages do not turn out to be what we expected when we exchanged our vows. Ask yourself the following questions:

YES NO

— — 1. Do you still love your spouse but feel that the spark has long since gone out?

— — 2. Do you ever feel if it weren't for your children, you might just pack your bags and go?

— — 3. Do you ever find yourself wondering 'is this all there is'?

— — 4. Do you find yourself looking at other younger couples and wishing you had what they have?

__ __   5. Do you find yourself thinking that marriage is not all it's cut out to be?

__ __   6. Do you have trouble remembering the last time you had fun or laughed with your spouse?

__ __   7. Do you listen to your married friends complain and wonder if anyone is happy?

__ __   8. Do you stay married only because of the horror stories you hear about being single?

__ __   9. Do you sometimes think that all your marriage is offering you is a minimum level of comfort?

__ __   10. Have you forgotten the last time your spouse said the words "I love you" with feeling?

__ __   11. Have you stopped using cute names to refer to each other?

__ __   12. Have you stopped looking forward to vacations or weekend outings together with excitement and anticipation?

__ __   13. Do you experience romance only through movies or a novel?

___ ___ 14. Do you sometimes feel you stay married for the financial

security?

___ ___ 15 Do you sometimes ask yourself if you've made a

mistake?

If you answered "yes" to several of these questions then you are

among the thousands of couples who are disenchanted in their marriage.

As a psychologist in private practice specializing in marriage therapy, I

hear these complaints very often. These are concerns voiced by those

partners who, for one of any number of reasons, choose to stay with

each other in an unhappy marriage.

Unfortunately, the fact that each person habitually complains is often

the one thing that the partnership still has in common. Most spouses do

not remember exactly when the tide started turning. That is because

except in the case of an affair there usually isn't a particularly traumatic

event. The disenchantment just seems to slowly creep into the marriage.

One day, you reflect on the past number of years and sadly realize that

things just are not the same, and this is not what you expected out of

your marriage. You would like it to be different - after all, your spouse is

not such a bad person.

As you reflect on the matter, different disheartening thoughts may come to mind; for example:

- "It's gone on for such a long time that it probably can't ever be any different;"

- "I have made my share of attempts, but it didn't seem to make any difference;"

- "There's never any time left in the day to do anything different;" or

- "There isn't really any extra money to get professional help."

But for sure, you do not have a clue what to do to make things better. After all, things were different when you got married - you were young, you were hopeful, you did not have all the responsibilities you have now. So perhaps you resign yourself to the hopeless belief that the dreams you had when you took your vows were just a fantasy, and now what you are living is the reality.

Well that's enough of the gloom and doom. How would you like to turn things around and put vitality, excitement, and romance back into your relationship? It can be done and I assure you I've seen it happen many times in my practice. But first, you need to ask yourself an all-important question:

"Do I feel my marriage is worth saving and do I truly want to make it work?"

It is essential that your answer to this question is a confident "YES!" You have to want this in order to find the energy and the motivation to shift out of many of the negative feelings you're experiencing right now. Only if you are sure that you are willing to try to save your marriage can you operate out of the positive mind-set that is necessary to make the changes or adjustments and rekindle those wonderful feelings the two of you had in the early days of your relationship. I suggest that you look at this book as a new adventure you and your partner are about to embark upon. I won't downplay the fact that it is going to take some extra effort. And there will be times you may have to put in more effort than your spouse to get him or her involved. But once you initiate this adventure, if you stay the course, the rewards at the end of the journey will be well worth the effort you put forth when you discover the excitement and romance are back. It *is* quite possible to put the vitality back into *your* marriage. Your marriage can be one that is satisfying to both you and your partner and one that brings joys to both of you.

There are actual tools that can be learned. Once applied, these skills bring your marriage back to life. Better yet, these tools are not difficult to learn. They are ones that everyone is capable of doing without the need for specialized training or a costly investment.

The only requirement is that you consistently commit to investing in and prioritizing your relationship. A marriage needs nurturing as a flower needs regular watering to thrive. The reason that you probably do not remember what went wrong, or when it went wrong, is because the marriage eroded slowly over time. The odds are you had the expectation that it would maintain itself while other issues took priority and ate up your time. Of course, at times, other things must take priority and a solid marriage can withstand occasional stress. But when "other issues" become the constant focus, the marriage cannot stay connected. If you have a good friend, you know that to keep the friendship going you must put some work into it. If neither person makes an effort toward that end, like calling or writing, to keep the connection, the friendship drifts. A marriage is no different.

In this book, you will find ways to reconnect with your partner. A person may have many different emotions in response to the relationship (s)he is in. In order to change something, a person needs to be aware of what it is they are experiencing. In each chapter, a different emotion will be identified. What the feeling is, and how it came about, is described.

Exercises are then offered in order to help you deal with the feeling, to become reconnected to your mate, and to revitalize your relationship.

Okay then, it looks like you're on your way to begin your adventure! Consider this book to be your partner as you set out, and realize you are *not* going into this alone. Any time we start something new, there is a bit of uncertainty - What will this be like?, How will I feel?, What will happen? Good questions to ask and the answers await you as you turn the pages. With each chapter you will unfold new discoveries, innovative approaches, and creative ways to practice what you've learned. This adventure has so much in store for you that you may find yourself unable to put the book down and will often come back to reread a passage. So prepare yourself to enjoy this enlightening experience. You deserve it!

HOW TO USE THIS BOOK

In my practice, it became obvious to me that though many couples did not choose to go the route of getting a divorce and adding to the already high 50% divorce rate, a good many of them were not happy. What also became apparent was that most of the couples shared some similarities – they weren't quite sure how the marriage got to the state it was in, they had a lot of uneasy but unidentified emotions, and they either did not have a clue or were too negative as to how to make things better.

These patterns started to keep showing up, and I realized they were similar to feelings I had experienced in my marriage. From this, a natural direction to the presentation of material unfolded. First, how does it happen that people can start out in a relationship with so many dreams and expectations, only to get to a point where there is such a discrepancy? Part I offers an explanation as to how this process happens.

Once in this situation, it is likely that there is a general sense of dissatisfaction, but many people are at a loss as to how to really get a handle on what's bothering them. It is my strong belief that it's hard to make a change - to get from one point to another - if you don't know where you are at the beginning of the process. You need to know how you feel to start on the road of changing your relationship. So, to offer guidance and direction in this area, Part II is devoted to identifying possible different emotions you may be experiencing. A different emotion is discussed in each new chapter. To achieve this clarification and offer an example of how that emotion might be expressed, each chapter starts out with a scenario of a dialogue between a couple. The scenarios, though perhaps not exact to something that has gone on in your life, typify the emotion being discussed. We then further elaborate on the feeling and how it might come about. Finally, in Section II, at the end of each chapter there is an exercise portion to help you to deal with the particular emotion.

Aside from individual feelings, there are some typical problems that arise in the way people communicate with each other. Couples in a marriage are especially prone to the fallout from poor communication since they are more vulnerable to one another. Clearly, many books on relationships offer suggestions on improving communication. However, many people do better at learning a skill when they understand the concepts behind them. Therefore, the first section of Part III helps the reader understand why poor communication occurs. The second section then deals with specific skills.

The first three sections are geared to working on the relationship. The order was based on a past, present, and future premise: how did it happen?, what do I feel now?, how can things be improved? But, as authors and professionals, we are aware that different people have varying needs and may be at different points in their process. Therefore, the book can be used in more individualized ways.

1) Some of you will want to read the whole book through, holding off on putting the exercises into practice, and just get a feel for what's going on.

2) Others of you may have a sense of how your relationship has deteriorated to the point it is at, but can't quite get a grip on exactly what you are feeling. In that case, you can go directly to Part II.

3) Still others may not be quite sure what exactly they are feeling. Each chapter in the Emotions Section is labeled. Read the scenario and

description; if it doesn't seem right, go to another one. Do keep in mind that you may feel more than one emotion at a time.

4) If you feel that the main problem in your relationship is a lack of communication, start with Section III. It will help you lay the groundwork for healthy and constructive dialogues. The information in this section will also assist you greatly with many of the Exercises in Section II.

5) Especially important in this book are the Exercises. The ones offered at the end of each emotion will help you deal with that particular feeling. Once you have a sense of what you are feeling, put the exercises into practice - whether you have stopped along the way or you have come back to them after reading the whole book.

It has been my experience as a therapist that a person can only *change him or herself – you cannot <u>expect</u> to get someone else to do something different. If you want something to <u>be</u> different, <u>you</u> have to <u>do</u> something different. You cannot try to make a situation change by getting the other person to change.* The responsibility is yours. It is most likely that the person who is more motivated to make a change *is the only one who is reading this book.* And it may seem unfair that you feel like, once again, you are the one who is doing something to make improvements. But there is good news. Generally, when one person initiates a change, this creates a new dynamic, and the other person will make changes, or adjustments, as a response. This is basic physics: "action=reaction."

Thus, as you familiarize yourself with the Exercises, you will notice that while they are designed for one person to initiate, they are meant (either directly or indirectly) to engage your partner in participating in the desired change. For example, let's say you are feeling shortchanged on the attention you are getting. Instead of just stewing about it, if you start showering your partner *with attention*, odds are this will eventually instill a desire in him or her to reciprocate.

A self-help book that responds to relationships must also be concerned with expressing feelings rather than just sucking it up and taking *all* of the responsibility. And, rightfully, you might ask, "Well, what if I have a certain feeling - how do I let my partner know?" The communication skills suggested in Part III are the ones that should be utilized for doing so.

As authors, we realize that many self-help books do not bring the promised rewards. Perhaps, you "worked" the book but it did not work for you. In Section IV, we respond to this concern.

In the pages that follow, we believe that we offer you a unique approach that will create a gratifying and fulfilling relationship with your mate. We wish you both happiness and joy.

PART ONE

ONE

WHAT HAPPENS WHEN YOU'RE IN A
STALEMATE WITH A STALE MATE?

Marriage, or a committed partnership, is a complicated, multi-faceted relationship. On a practical level, such a relationship has many good points that allow it to function well. As an example, it is generally easier from a financial perspective to be involved with a partner; that is expenses like the rent, the electric bill and the groceries are shared. Additionally, partners may choose a "hunter-gatherer" lifestyle. That is, one person brings in all or most of the money while the other person maintains the household tasks.

Traditionally, men tended to be the "bread-winners" (hunters) and women the "task-doers" (gatherers). This arrangement was very efficient in that the man could earn as much money as possible because he didn't have to worry about the laundry, the errands, the cleaning, the cooking.

Similarly, since the woman did not have to worry about how she'd earn the money to pay the bills, she could focus on maintaining the household.

But nowadays, most couples do not function in such a traditional way. There is a shared responsibility for earning money, many times equally by each partner. As women have taken on a greater part of the financial contribution, in exchange, they expect men to share in the household tasks. Regardless of the arrangement chosen, it is usually easier to function as a couple than as a single person. In an effort toward having the partnership run smoothly, a pattern generally becomes established. This pattern will reflect who does what task, as well as when and how the task gets done. Regardless of the unique pattern that each couple may establish, what is common to all couples is having some sort of a routine. Routine, by definition, implies consistency and predictability. When human beings have consistent and predictable routines, by nature, they experience comfort and safety.

In addition to the routines of daily living, there will also be typical ways to acknowledge the special events in a couple's life. Such things include birthdays, holidays, or memorable occasions. Again, there may be variation from one couple to another but across the board what couples strive for are meaningful times that bring a sense of joy, belonging, and connection.

Another aspect that a marriage offers is having a partner with whom to share the more common events in your life. Events can range from having someone to pick you up when your car is being serviced, to going to the movies, or out to dinner.

Most likely, you and your partner have established certain patterns so that your marriage "functions." But as positive as the idea is that your marriage functions, herein also lies a problem. Functioning is machine-like. And, in fact, the very aspects that allow the marriage to be functional are the same ones potentially leading to its downfall. For most of you who are reading this book, your marriage has become stale. While the functioning aspect of it may be efficient, it is not necessarily emotionally rewarding, joyful, satisfying, or passionate.

When a marriage becomes stale, it is a long process rather than something that happens overnight. For the purposes of contrast, suppose your partner got into a car accident and became paralyzed. Certainly, major changes would occur in your partner's life and yours. But you would be able to easily point to the event responsible for the change. Stale marriages, like food, become bad over time. Let's think about cheese as an example. One day you open the fridge, you look at the cheese and notice mold. You realize that the process of deterioration has been occurring.

- Similarly, have you become aware of the feeling that there's just no more "umph" in your relationship?

- Do you find that you're no longer excited to see your partner, or to spend time with each other?

- When Friday night comes, signaling the upcoming weekend, do you feel like there's nothing you really look forward to?

- Even when you *do* have the time to spend together, do you either experience the sense of being tuned out, or feel yourself tuning out the other person? In general, is the relationship sort of on "automatic pilot?" - is it functioning but with no enjoyment or passion? Like the cheese, has your relationship deteriorated? If so, you are in a stalemate with a stale mate.

TWO

WOMAN OR MAN CANNOT LIVE BY
EXPECTATIONS ALONE

When we get involved in anything, there are always expectations that we have about the situation or person. Remember as you progressed from childhood to being an adult, the array of expectations that cropped up: What will going to camp be like?, What kind of paper do I have to write to get a good grade?, What will my blind date be like?, How will my new friend and I get along?

The expectations we hold are the result of many different sources of input, such as: what we were taught by our parents, how we saw our parents and other significant people act, the influence of the media, and our own wants and needs. These expectations act as filtering systems that allow us to make assessments and adjust our feelings and behaviors accordingly. For instance, you may expect that a good friend will have no problem changing his or her plans to be with you when you tell them you have a personal crisis. You've come to that expectation because you saw how your family handled similar situations. That is, if someone was in dire need, that person's problem came above anything else and if someone did not respond similarly, your family expressed hurt. If your friend does meet your expectation, you are pleased and feel good about him or her. If, however, your friend was brought up with different values (s)he may not want to change plans even if you are in a personal crisis. Undoubtedly, you will feel hurt and perhaps believe that your needs are unimportant to this person. Further, you may end up expressing your hurt feelings, either directly or indirectly. The problem with expectations is that they are very egocentric. We behave consistently with our expectations, unaware that other people may have different perceptions from ours. It is important to realize that these perceptions are merely *different*, not necessarily right or wrong.

Perhaps one of the biggest issues that I have consistently come across in relationships is the expectation that "the other person will be just like me." Even more damaging is the idea that "if they aren't like me and cannot understand my needs, they don't care about or love me." A consequence of this perception, and one that is often unrecognized, is the belief that the person we marry *will* be able to, as well as *should* be able to meet *all* of our needs. After all, this is our one true love. Though when challenged, most people will acknowledge that this is unrealistic, there is a subconscious expectation which leads to a level of dissatisfaction. Even though the origination of the feeling is unconscious, women, having been raised to be more in touch with their feelings, are more prone to experience this dissatisfaction.

The other major expectation, which usually is held by each partner, is that we will get married and "will live happily ever after." A primary contributor to this belief is the result of how love is portrayed in the media. We read books, watch movies, and listen to songs that often portray *happiness* when we are *with* someone, and *desperation* when we are *without* someone. When we're in love, everything is right in the world; so, "all you need is love." Prince Charming comes along and carries his love off on his white horse - they go galloping into the sunset and live happily ever after. Such nice endings make us feel good at the time, but we forget that they are the products of writers' imaginations. They are fantasies which present an image that could not be any further from the truth. "Happily ever after" is not something that we can expect to just happen. In reality "happily ever after" is the result of prioritizing your relationship and paying attention to how you communicate, both verbally and nonverbally. Your fairytale does not have to be just a fantasy.

THREE

VARIETY CAN BE THE SPICE OF LIFE

Unlike the high school driver's education classes we took long ago, courses on marriage are only starting to be offered. We learn about marriage mostly through our parents (or the dominant people in our lives), observing the way they did it. Sometimes, when we are aware of aspects in our parents' relationship that we don't like, we make a conscious effort to do things differently. Still, the tools for knowing what will work best are not readily at our disposal.

One of the cruelest realities is that saying the words "I love you," in and of itself, will not be enough to sustain a relationship. For a while, it may be. There may be an initial period where the novelty of marriage will help carry the couple along. How novel the marriage is will vary. Factors such as how long the couple has been together, whether they have lived together prior to marriage, and long held expectations will all impact the initial phase of being married. This is the "honeymoon" period and is similar in dynamics to the honeymoon phase of a new relationship. There is newness, there is a sense of enthusiasm, and there is a positive emotional filtering system. Though the time frame may vary as to how long this period lasts, eventually, it ends. And so, eventually the honeymoon is over.

The very fact that the couple is made up of two different people usually from different backgrounds presents a challenge. This can be true even if the couple has very similar backgrounds regarding such things as religion, race, socioeconomic status, and geographic location. The actual upbringing was done in two different families who, more likely than not, did things differently. Things like how birthdays were celebrated, how chores were done, and how finances were handled, will vary. But two people do not have to be exactly alike in order for a relationship to function. However, they do have to understand and accept that these differences exist. Through acceptance of these differences there is a greater likelihood that either person will not experience being let down by the other.

John Gray, in his book, "Men Are From Mars, Women Are From Venus," makes us very aware of gender differences. Again, these differences reflect a different way of looking at the world and consequential behaviors, due to upbringing and expected roles for the genders. Perhaps one of the major complaints I have found in my own practice is the feeling that the other spouse "does not understand." Upon further examination, the "lack of understanding" (and feeling that one is not loved) is really nothing more than these different worldviews experienced by men and women.

Another reality that is often overlooked is the fact that people express themselves differently. This can happen for a number of reasons. Given that people have been raised in various backgrounds, they may or may not discuss their feelings openly. For those who are uncomfortable with self-expression or do not feel secure enough asking for what they want, speaking indirectly or dropping hints may be the preferred choice. Even when the feelings are positive, they may still be expressed less directly. Some people will perform small acts of kindness; others will express greater affection. Though there are exceptions, men are often less verbal and like to get to the "bottom line"; women tend to need greater verbal interchange. And, to further complicate matters, people may use different modalities to communicate. A person may speak and/or listen in ways that favor visual, auditory, or tactile references. As an example, following the same order just mentioned, a person might say either, "I don't see a problem," or "I don't hear the problem," or "I don't sense a problem." Though all of this may seem a bit overwhelming, it really isn't. But it requires an awareness of the differences and an ability to see them as just that - differences. Nothing more. Nothing less.

A partnership will naturally encounter stress. There are the normal tugs of day-to-day living - extended families, flat tires, tension at work, or sickness. Finances often present a common source of pressure. Is there enough money to do all that is wanted? Does the couple handle finances similarly? On what expenses should the money be allocated? Though not intentionally, all of these concerns can tug at the couple. Couples will encounter small hassles as a part of everyday living. Even in the absence of conflicts between the couple in responding to these normal stresses, time and energy is expended. With only so much time and energy to go around, attending to the relationship may get put on the "back burner." So, these small struggles may unintentionally add up, resulting in a not-so-small impact on the relationship.

Most marriages include children. Certainly, they bring joy and add love to the family unit. But, often, on a day-to-day basis, children also add stress. There are that many more people and personalities with whom to contend. Additionally, the relationships between the siblings can be difficult. And, of course, for most families, there is the need for greater financial security. Having children creates changes in the way a relationship functions. Certainly, who the couple is and how they function with one another will be quite different before having children, during child-raising, and after children leave the home. Each new phase will require attention, awareness, and probably a re-balancing. Research has indicated that the most vulnerable periods for divorce to occur are:

1) within the first seven years when couples are adjusting to one another

2) starting to have children and

3) again when couples are raising teenagers (Gottman, 2000).

Another reality which may present itself as a potential "trap" in a marriage is that we forget, or do not realize, that people have traits that by nature are complex. That is, a common characteristic of a person is to have both an "up" side and a "down" side. We fall in love with a person's "up" side: "I love that he takes charge and makes all the plans for the evening." But that very same "take charge attitude" years down the road, when the honeymoon is over, may well bring out feelings of being controlled; feelings that no longer are experienced as romantic. Another example is the man who marries a woman because he feels so comfortable with her that she reminds him of his mother. As time passes, he comes to lose romantic interest, or even resent her because she is, in fact, too much like his mother. Though nobody is perfect, it is important to be aware that this "down" side exists and not be naively enamored by the "up" side. Being aware of who your partner is allows you to avoid having unrealistic expectations only to be disheartened down the road.

It is an unfair assumption to think that the role each partner assumed at the beginning of the relationship will remain constant throughout it. A relationship goes through a natural evolution and is vulnerable to various stressors. In order to adapt to stressors, there may be shifts in each of the partner's personalities. Or, potential shifts may also be the consequence of either partner's personal growth. Either because of particular stressors or because of the changes made by one of the partners on a more personal level, different roles and behaviors may now become appropriate. Through the years, new needs and wants may surface. It is essential that these differences and changes be embraced within the relationship. Awareness, sharing, and nurturing of one another allows for the fluidity of a relationship rather than a sense of boredom and anxiety. And later in this book you will be given the tools with which to make this happen.

FOUR

WORKIN' 9-5...AND THEN SOME

Even under the best of circumstances, marriages are really put to a test. If hypothetically, a couple had similar backgrounds, pretty much saw things from the same perspective, and did not have too much of their own baggage, you might think they'd had it made. But life is complex and does not run according to a set-in-stone plan. Even in marriages where the partners are responsible and caring people, problems and demands are likely to occur and must be addressed.

As an example, let's say that you had Monday night set up to just kick back and relax. Your oldest child comes home with a math assignment that he just cannot understand. He works on it for a while and then comes to you. Are you going to dismiss him and continue watching TV with your spouse or offer some help? It has probably been a long time since you have done algebra so you are rusty in explaining it to him. Not only have you given up your time to work with him but now, there is also tension because the help session is not going so well. There goes your relaxing Monday night. Luckily, due to the modern advances of technology, you are able to tape the show you wanted to watch and being a flexible person, you plan to watch it together on Tuesday. Then you remember that on Tuesday night there is an important PTA meeting that you feel is necessary to attend. Oh well, Wednesday it is. Wednesday night comes, all the chores are done, and you and your spouse sit down and turn on the VCR. Two minutes into the opening credits, suddenly there are loud noises from upstairs. You give it a minute as you hold your breath. The noises become louder as your two youngest children race into the den, each complaining and yelling about the other. Naturally, this needs your attention. Oh well, there's always Friday night. No wait, you just remembered...

Sound familiar? The problem is that this scenario is not only familiar but also goes on night after night, week after week, month after month. Unintentionally, without awareness, you have ignored your relationship with your spouse. Maybe the particulars are different in your situation, but the net result is the same. Most of us put "quality time with our spouse" on a back burner. We assume that it can wait; we assign other things as more important. But that can only go on for so long. Eventually the camel's back breaks!

A key element that is often missing in a couple's understanding of their relationship is that in order to have a good relationship, it requires ongoing attention. A satisfying, positive relationship does not just happen. In order for a good relationship to exist, it must be a work-in-progress relationship. Though we tend to think of marriage as a relationship primarily based on emotional interactions, to respond purely through emotions, puts the marriage at risk. In fact, a marriage requires work. Often the concept of "work" in reference to a relationship sounds like a dirty word. After all, haven't you been working all day? A lot has been written about the differences in styles of men and women as it pertains to the need for, and ability to, express themselves emotionally. No doubt, this is a main component of the "work" that is necessary in a solid relationship. Yet, there is a simpler concept that too often gets overlooked and that is, giving the relationship *priority*. Working at making sure there is time for the two of you. Wouldn't it be nice if it were as simple as the Beatles would have us believe when they sang, "All ya' need is love." Love is a good beginning - but it is only a starting point. Just as a plant dies without the presence of sun and water, so will a relationship

wither in the absence of ongoing attention and nurturing.

I am not suggesting that all your time needs to be spent together. In a

healthy relationship, each partner may want or need to do his or her own

thing. How much private time each person requires will depend on the

individuals and their particular needs.

In today's world, many couples find themselves in very demanding

and stressful lifestyles, usually due to economical reasons. For others, it

may be a factor such as a choice involving career enhancement.

Regardless of the reason, though many couples can cope with the stresses

of day-to-day living, there are residual consequences, such as tiredness,

frustration, and irritability. And often, when we are so stressed we tend

to pay more attention to our own needs and wants, almost with a sense

of entitlement. We become numb to the stress and numb to its impact

on our relationship.

Obviously, there are many times when things will happen that could

not be predicted, and temporary re-prioritizing is necessary.

Unfortunately, there also may be situations that will demand large time

commitments, and will become disruptive. If, for example, one partner's

parent takes ill, attention to the parent's health may have to come before all else. If one person in the relationship has a deadline on a big project

for work, the other may have to give up shared time and/or pick up the

slack in running the household. These commitments are unexpected, but

necessary, "evils." If a relationship is solid, it can maintain itself through

stressful, difficult times. But to assume that the relationship will always

be there will be a grave mistake. If we get sloppy about taking care of

our relationship, one day there may be no relationship to come back to.

FIVE

STAYING THE COURSE WHEN THE ROAD GETS ROCKY

No doubt, there are times that things seem so dull, so boring that you wonder to yourself, "Can this possibly be all there is to marriage?" Perhaps, you have even gone further and fantasized that some other person and a different relationship would make you happier. You may even realize that you, yourself, had something to do with this sorry state of affairs. So, if you could just start all over, you would not make the same mistakes. After all, life is short and you are entitled to some happiness.

Of course, we are *all* entitled to some joy and happiness. But that satisfaction does not automatically come by merely disentangling from this relationship and starting all over again. Divorce, even in its best-case scenario, is a devastating and stressful process on each partner. It is not the purpose of this book to go over the harsh, difficult facts about what the consequences of divorce do to you and the children. We have all read about how divorce takes a toll on children (socially, academically, and emotionally). These consequences go beyond immediate manifestations. There are long-term scars resulting in difficulties in their adult relationships. Also, divorce, as a means to solve the problem, becomes the role model for the children.

Joyous occasions such as holidays and special events (like graduation and birthdays) become fraught with tension, due to the children's keen awareness of the rift. Children experience guilt about potentially divided loyalties.

In the best of marriages, finances are a source of potential difficulty. Factor in divorce, and finance becomes a main source of disagreement. A good deal of the emotional bitterness between the couple gets channeled into this area. Of course, divorce by its very meaning, requires the set up of a second household. For most people, the financial picture is a strained one for all involved. So, aside from the emotional tugs, there is also a dramatic change in lifestyle.

The fantasy of the good life that one would have when unencumbered by a lifeless marriage is, unfortunately, usually just that - a fantasy. Perhaps, initially, there's a great sense of freedom because of feeling a sense of relief. However, just about all reports I hear from people who have chosen to leave their relationship is that the single life is a hard and lonely existence, not nearly as exciting as they expected. It's very hard to meet people. The people that they do meet often turn out to be "losers." They have a date they thought went well, only to never hear from the person again. Or, they get deeply involved only to discover too late that the *new person* is just like their "ex." It's a sad comment on our singles society that many people are able to put up a good front just long enough to hook someone in. Then, like Dr. Jeckle, the Mr. Hyde personality suddenly creeps in. I can't tell you how many times I've heard a divorced dater complain, along the lines of, "I don't understand what happened. (S)He was so nice and considerate during the courting phase. Now it seems that all (s)he cares about is her-/himself."

Perhaps, the most significant reason to stay and work on the marriage is the fact that a new relationship will not necessarily solve the problem. A new relationship is exciting and fun (something similar to the feelings you once had with your partner in the relationship you have ended). You and your new partner are learning about each other and exploring the newness. You think of the other person and get a warm feeling all over. You actually cannot wait until the time that you can spend together.

Each of you makes efforts to let the other know you are thinking about them. A real effort to be considerate is made by each of you to be concerned and aware of the other. What a great time - the honeymoon. But without the tools, there is no reason to assume that things will be any different from your former relationship. When that flower starts withering, if you do not know the proper way to take care of it, it will die - even if it is a new and different flower.

SIX

THE GOOD NEWS

Not only can most marriages be saved, but also they can return to the original beginnings that were vibrant, joyful, and brought happiness to each partner. Eighty percent of couples who remain in troubled marriages report being happy five years later (Waite, 2000). You may think this is not possible, but that is only because you do not yet know the steps to achieve this (which we will get into later). A marriage needs focused attention and to be treated with respect. There is really only one thing you have to commit to and that is a willingness to make the effort: to make your partnership a priority, to give it the same attention you do your children, business, or friends. If you are reading this book, then it is safe to assume that you are already at some level of disappointment or despair. But those same feelings can be transformed into delight and a sense of harmony. But the only way for this "magical" change to take place is to make a commitment. Start...now!

No doubt, some of you have reservations. That is understandable. You may feel that this sorry state of affairs has gone on too long and that there is too much water under the bridge. Should this be the case, then it may, in fact, take a little longer for the process to work for you, or it may require a little more effort. On the other hand, sometimes when something has been missing for so long, the shift is such a welcome one that you responded to it very quickly. Others of you will say that you really have a strong desire to make things work, but there is no way that you can picture your spouse reading this book, let alone making an effort to change. The advantage of the tools that are offered is that *both* partners do *not* have to actively work on the problem. The results can absolutely be attained if at least one partner is willing to start trying. The reason for this is that when one partner starts to do something differently, the routine is broken (whatever that routine is). The other partner, in response, will then do something different. Thus, one of you starting the "reaction" will automatically be the catalyst for the other to join in on the fun.

One of the definitions of insanity is to think that you can keep doing things the same way and yet expect something different to happen. If you *want* something different to happen, then you have to *do* something different. Well, how do you know that your partner's reaction to your change will be a positive one? The suggestions made in this book are all based on a positive outlook, and working toward getting things going in a constructive way. Now, I have often heard one partner say that it is not fair for them to make changes if their partner is not going to do likewise. Sadly, the other partner feels the same way. Each person in the relationship is experiencing any number of feelings that stand in the way of either wanting to take a step, to put forth some effort. But if they both feel this way, hurt, righteous in their withholding, and waiting for the other to make a move, the only result is that the relationship remains in a stuck mode, in a stalemate. You need to ask yourself what your goal is. You can certainly make the choice to wait for your partner to make the first move. Unfortunately, this attitude is going to be your loss and may result in your loneliness. By taking the first step, it moves you and the relationship *out* of being stuck and onto a forward moving path that can bring you both a sense of satisfaction and enjoyment.

Finally, some of you may have been down so long that it does not feel like there are any real feelings or passion for your partner. You see your mate as a responsible husband or wife, good parent, and decent human being. But that's where it stops. It is hard to believe you ever called this person a "cutie." The truth for most of us is that the feelings are still there - just buried under lots of responsibilities, tiredness, and confusion. As you start to pay more attention to your partner, they will start to come to life. And so will the old loving feelings.

PART TWO

INTRODUCTION

Let's say you are at a huge mall that you've never been to before and you want to get to a particular store. Well, it's great to know where you want to go, but you also need to know your starting point. Without knowing where you are, it is very difficult to know how to get to where you want to be. So you need to know "You Are Here" on the mall map.

A relationship is clearly more complicated than a mall map and takes in more sensitive matters. But because a partnership is so vulnerable to sensitive concerns, the more it can be understood, the greater the chance it will be satisfying. How can you reach your goal of having a meaningful relationship if you don't know where you stand in it initially? And if the terrain is rough, it is especially vital to know where you are as you start off on your journey.

The section that follows, Part II, is to help you identify your emotions. At first, that may sound silly. But many people do not instantly recognize that they are feeling upset or negative. Others may sense that they are not happy but don't really have a good handle on what it is they're feeling. It is hard to communicate productively if you can't even speak about your own experience. Relationships, especially those that are not functioning well, are hard enough to deal with. The more that can be understood, the greater the chance that the partnership you want can be created.

Each chapter is labeled as a different emotion. If you think you know what you're feeling, you can go directly to that emotion. The dialogue at the beginning of each chapter is a way to illustrate the kind of conversation that might go on with a couple caught up in the named emotion. The description that follows, gives a greater conceptual understanding. If you can relate to the material, work on the exercises that are offered for that emotion. Keep in mind that it is likely that you could be experiencing more than one emotion.

If you are not sure of what you are feeling, start to read each chapter and see if it fits. If it doesn't reflect how you feel, go on to the next one.

This part of the book is set up to offer you flexibility. You can identify all the emotions that relate to you initially and then go back to the pertinent exercises. Or, you can work with one emotion at a time. Pace your approach in a way that feels right to you. The main idea is to stay mindful and focused about doing the exercises and remembering the concepts, in order to have the relationship you want.

In the following pages you will find the different emotions that you might be experiencing. Which ones can you relate to? Remember to identify the feeling and do the exercises at the end of the pertinent one(s). Don't forget that you can work on one at a time or find all the appropriate ones first before you proceed to do the exercises.

UNDERSTANDING EMOTIONS

Usually when we think about improving communication, it almost always involves "listening" to what *others* are saying, or perhaps feeling. While there is certainly merit to this, what sometimes tends to be overlooked is the importance of "listening to *ourselves.*" This may not be as difficult as it sounds. Our bodies are generally giving us messages or signals all the time. Consider if you will, the following examples: we've all heard of "women's instinct," "gut reaction," or "having a hunch." For some of us, this may show up negatively as "that nagging ache," "butterflies in our stomach," or "that persistent lethargy." This chapter addresses two essential areas: understanding some of the physical "triggers" to our feelings as well as identifying the emotions we sometimes experience. Learning about these issues will help you see that first of all, you are not alone, and secondly there is a way to get a handle on these issues.

Many times, when we think about feeling an emotion, we realize that there are particular sensations that we feel in our body. Different people may feel different things. Though any number of bodily parts can experience an emotion, many people tend to feel it in their backs, stomachs, throats, chest, or head. In fact, some people are more readily aware of the sensation that they experience in their body, rather than intellectually knowing that they are feeling some emotion. In reality, there is lots of research to indicate that there are not separate sensations for separate emotions. For example, anger does not come out in the head and hurt in the stomach. The body has a biological activation system that responds to stress. That system goes into effect regardless of which particular emotion is being felt. It is a way of alerting you to the fact that something is bothering you. Depending on the particulars, we label the feelings accordingly. As an example, if you feel left out, you will label the emotion neglect. Or, if you believe you are not being heard, you might label the emotion misunderstood. The most important thing is for you to become aware of what you are experiencing (physiologically as well as emotionally). Nothing can be dealt with unless you are aware that something is bothering you. So, when you can identify a particular feeling/emotion or a physical sensation (e.g. migraine headache, back discomfort, etc.), it is a good beginning and may well be an important first step in paying attention to yourself.

ONE

DISAPPOINTED AND DISILLUSIONED

Scenario 1

Sue has been working under some stressful situations with her current employer and is grappling with internal politics revolving around moving up the corporate ladder.

SUE: The weekend can't get here too soon as far as I'm concerned.

BOB: Having another one of those weeks again?

SUE: No kidding! I can't believe the politics that go on day-in-and-day-out. It's a wonder I get any work done.

BOB: Dear, it's just a job and why do you get so hooked into it?

SUE: But, it's not just a job for me. By now you should know it's part of who I am. If anyone should understand that, it's you.

BOB: I *do* understand, Sue. I'm just saying that putting all your energy into it isn't the most productive behavior, that's all.

SUE: Oh, so now you think I'm not being productive. Is that it? So, how would you handle the situation?

BOB: Well, I'd probably roll with the flow and try to lighten things up a little bit. Maybe you're not putting things in perspective.

SUE: Is that a "guy" thing...rolling with the flow? So, you think the "good old boy" mentality is just something I should learn to put up with. Have I got it right?

BOB: Look, Sue, I'm just pointing out there are always two sides to a situation and maybe you're not seeing both because you're too emotional right now.

SUE: Unbelievable! I really can't believe you're not taking my side in this crap I have to put up with. There used to be a time you really understood me and I could count on you to stand by me. Some *help* you've turned out to be!

BOB: Jeez! I thought I *was* being helpful.

SUE: You call taking *their* side *being helpful?* God I feel so disappointed in you right now!

Half of all marriages end up in a divorce. This is a well-known statistic (Kelleher, 2000). It would be hard to imagine that anyone is completely impervious to all of the well-publicized negativity about marriage and divorce. Today, people are getting married later. This age-delayed phenomenon is occurring for a number of reasons, with apprehension regarding the benefits of marriage being one of them. Many are offspring of parents who have divorced. Yet, for these men and women, as well as those from intact families, hope continues to shine through. Marriage is still an institution in which most of us still believe. Year after year, wedlock is entered into with all sorts of plans and dreams. Some folks are not married and do not wish to be, but most believe that there is something lacking in their life if they are not in a partnership. And so, when the "right" one (or nearly the "right" one) comes along, we move forward in an attempt to create harmony, satisfaction, and joy.

We continue to marry and bring into the relationship all our dreams and expectations. Though we may be aware that 50% of all marriages fail, we like to think ours will be different. We will always be friends with our partner and we will lovingly share our thoughts and emotions with them. Support in any number of varied ways will be there for one another. Struggles that may come will be mere bumps in the journey. We will be able to look to one another for relief from stress, and enjoy shared good times. And, of course, we will always sit next to each other at social functions unlike all those other couples that after years of marriage, sit across the room from one another, barely acknowledging one another's existence.

These statements reflect the more obvious expectations. Based on the way we are raised, there are also likely to be more subtle beliefs that will have profound implications in your marriage. These beliefs are so ingrained that we may be unaware of them. For some, we expect our partner to be everything to us. Our mate is to be our friend, lover, supporter, playmate, helper, and so on. Our mate surely will not only know what we need, but also when and how we need it as well, right?

Though you may think that this attitude is demanding, think about your own relationship. You say you realize that no one person can be everything to another. Yet, when your spouse is not available in the way you would like, an uneasy, dissatisfied feeling comes up.

- "Why doesn't she understand that I need a night out with the guys?"
- "How come he forgot to get me a card for our anniversary?"
- "Why, when I just need a hug, does he keep offering solutions?"
- "Can't she wait till I've relaxed from a day's work to start complaining about the kids?"
- "Why, when I talk to my friends do they get it, but my spouse doesn't?"

Perhaps the first few times, you are able to overlook your discontent - maybe your spouse is having a bad day, maybe your partner for life did not realize you needed something, maybe the kids required attention.

For most people, you cannot even put your finger on exactly what is wrong or when things started to be so disappointing. Yet, after years of commitment, you can clearly recognize that you do feel disappointed and disillusioned. Of course, there is the necessary career or careers. Some of you enjoy, except for periodic bad days, what you do. But most people work hard so that they can manage all the financial obligations and often do not find their job to bring challenge, stimulation, and enjoyment. The weekend comes (weeknights usually do not offer much down time) and you look forward to relaxation, renewal of strength, and reconnection to your emotional support system. Yet, the weekend sometimes offers different stresses and obligations. Johnny's game, Lisa's recital along with the uniforms, fund-raisers, and of course, the endless carpooling. The weekend tasks may vary in specifics but the feeling of pressure they exert on you never lets up. You or your mate is lost somewhere in the fog of family busyness and if you can manage to connect with one another, it is not nearly in the way you had hoped.

You come to your mate for all those good things you anticipated in your marriage. Somehow, she or he is not always responsive, or the response given does not feel all that helpful. Her actions and ways of behaving are far different from what you had originally thought she was like. Where are the little acts of kindness or the bigger sense of creature comfort you originally derived from being in a partnership? So, after all this time, you find yourself asking, "Is this all there is?"

Disappointed and Disillusioned Exercises:

1a. For this exercise, you will need to make two columns. In one column, make a list of the behaviors that your mate exhibits that disappoint you. In the other column, make a list of behaviors your mate exhibits that please you.

As you look at the two columns, make a comparison to help you gain a better perspective of your situation.

- Do the positive traits outweigh the negative ones?

- Even if there are more traits listed on the negative side, do you feel the ones on the positive side are more important?

- Think about the ways in which you and your partner were raised; reconsider that the negative traits are really a reflection of a difference in your upbringings rather than a disappointment.

Also, write down the attributes you expected in your mate and again consider whether those expectations are realistic given your mate's background.

If after going through this personal evaluation, there are traits that still leave you feeling disappointed or disillusioned, it is time to raise them with your partner. (Effective communication skills are presented later in the book. It is important to remember to not attack your partner but to raise those things that are disturbing to you objectively.)

1b. For special events like holidays, birthdays, and anniversaries, talk to your partner about what each of you expects.

Each of you takes a turn at finishing this sentence: "My idea of a meaningful anniversary (or whichever occasion you want to discuss) is…"

Since unspoken assumptions often lead to disappointment, be sure each of you gets to express your needs. Then see what you have in common as well as where there are differences.

Come up with some compromise to reconcile the differences, e.g. a third option that suits both of you or a decision to do things according to one's wishes one year and the other partner's, the following year.

TWO

DISRESPECTED AND DISREGARDED

Scenario 2

Sue and Bob are catching a quick breakfast on the run, as they both are getting ready to head out to their respective jobs.

BOB: I went ahead and told my boss that we'll be at his dinner party this weekend, so don't forget, okay?

SUE: What dinner party this weekend? I thought we agreed we were spending the weekend with my folks.

BOB: Sue, you said that was next weekend, I'm sure.

SUE: What do you mean you're sure? Because I definitely said *this* weekend. They're expecting us and I don't want to let them down.

BOB: Now come on, you know I can't let my boss down either. This is more important.

SUE: I'm sure it's important to you, but why didn't you check with me first?

BOB: I'm almost positive I did, which is why I went ahead and said we'd be there. Can't you just tell your parents something came up and we'll see them the following weekend.

SUE: But that's unfair, Bob! Lately it seems *everything* revolves around you and your darn job.

BOB: Now that's an exaggeration. We frequently do stuff you've planned. Just this once I'm asking you to bend a little.

SUE: Bend a little? I feel like all I do is bend over backwards to meet your needs. My parents really need our help with their annual garage sale this weekend and I'd feel terrible if they had to move all that stuff in and out by themselves. So this is really a priority to me. Can't you politely get out of the dinner party, just this once?

BOB: They did it without us last year.

SUE: That's why I feel so bad - we'd be deserting them twice in a row.

BOB: I don't know, Sue. I just don't think you get the *real* priority here.

As you first started dating, you took great care to think about the other person. You were concerned that the restaurant you wanted to go to served food the other person liked. You suggested two or three different movies that you were interested in and asked your partner which of the options they found most appealing. If some change in plan had to occur, you made sure to let the other person know. These types of considerations are considered as being respectful to one another. Usually, as a relationship evolves and each of the partners feels more comfortable with one another, there is less formality and greater latitude in dealing with each other. However, this does not mean that the need for mutual respect no longer exists.

Each relationship will create a balance that is unique to it. That is, the particulars of how each partner gives to each other may vary. Some couples function traditionally with the woman taking care of all the household needs and the man being responsible for bringing in the money. Others will divide the workload evenly. Or, responsibilities can be shared in a fluid manner whereby tasks are done depending on needs at any given time; for instance, more of the load is carried by one partner if the other is laid up or involved in a particularly busy time at work. Variation in what is given may also have to do with the kind of support that is offered; some partners are able to offer emotional assistance and others are stronger in problem-solving ways. The specifics are not as important as a sense that the relationship is reciprocally satisfying.

You went into this relationship feeling that you would derive a mutual benefit from it. Each of you felt invested in the relationship and secure that this was true of your mate. Suddenly, you become aware of the fact that your partner forgets to call when going to be late. Or, something has happened during the day that is really upsetting; yet, there does not seem to be any time where you sense that your partner is really listening to you. If your partner does sit down to listen, it is only in a preoccupied manner. There seem to be endless additional tasks necessary to get ready for holiday preparation. The event is important to both of you, but your partner offers no additional assistance.

It seems the relationship has begun to function perfunctorily. The concern for one another is dramatically absent. You start to feel a great sense of disregard and disrespect. And you certainly do not feel that the relationship is reciprocal or as satisfying as it was in the beginning.

Disrespected and Disregarded Exercises:

2a. Ask about your partner. Show interest.

Ask your mate in the morning what kind of day (s)he has planned. Then afterwards, jot anything down you can remember (such as an important meeting or a doctor's appointment). At the end of the day, look back at this list and when your mate comes home, ask him or her how the meeting or medical appointment went. When your partner appears to be finished talking, make a simple request like, "tell me more." Be sure to maintain good eye contact while listening and try to actively listen by occasionally paraphrasing what your partner said. You can say something like, "It sounds like your meeting was very productive and some important decisions were made." This will ensure you really did follow the story.

2b. If your partner has shared something with you, follow-up on it a few days later by asking about it. Again, it may help to make a written note about what they've shared to help you remember to ask about it. You can note this on a calendar, notepad, or in a journal. Also, it will assist you to think about what questions you'll ask. Try to use open-ended questions that start with words such as "what, when, where, why, who, or how." By using questions like, "What was the outcome of your meeting with your boss?" you give your mate a chance to say as much as they'd like and open up the conversation.

2c. If you are going to ask about your partner, do it at a time when you can really pay attention. Do not attempt to show your interest while trying to get dinner on the table or help the kids with homework. Also, try to minimize other distractions such as the phone, pager, TV, or the stereo being too loud. One way to approach this is to set aside time for "the two of you" on a regular basis. This "two of you time" can be anywhere from 15 minutes to an hour, depending on your schedules that day. The important thing is that you both make a commitment to have this be a priority. This is a time to catch up with one another without interruptions or distractions (e.g. put the answering machine on, turn off the TV).

2d. If your mate has a doctor's appointment, ask about it. (It may be hard to remember with so many things going on. Helpful hint - mark it in your calendar.) Remember to use open-ended questions like "How did your doctor's appointment go?" or say, "I'm very interested in knowing the outcome of your medical appointment. Would you like to tell me about it?"

2e. If you realize you have a little extra time and your mate is busy, do one of the chores (s)he usually does. As an example, let's say your mate typically takes out the garbage. You can surprise him or her by doing it for them. Another option is to let your mate know you'd like to make his or her day easier and ask, "What can I take care of for you today to give you a break?"

2f. Be willing to try an activity that your partner likes by either not objecting to it or making the initiative on your own. So, for example, if your mate enjoys golfing and you've never participated, you might ask when (s)he next plan to golf and offer to tag along and perhaps get a mini-lesson. Another approach would be to offer to go to a movie that you know (s)he is dying to see but wouldn't be on your top ten list. It's all about showing interest in and respect for your mate.

THREE

WORN OUT

Scenario 3

Bob and Sue have just gotten into bed and are watching the news on television. Sue is reading and just closed her book and begins to go to sleep. A few moments later Bob turns off the news, shuts the light and snuggles up to Sue, beginning to embrace her and lightly kiss her neck.

BOB: I love you, sweetie.

SUE: (sleepily) Love you too, Bob.

BOB: I've missed being close with you, honey (continuing to kiss and stroke Sue's face).

SUE: (unresponsive to Bob's caresses) Uh-huh.

BOB: You feeling okay, hon? You're not sick, are you?

SUE: No, I'm just really sleepy and it's late.

BOB: C'mon, honey. It's not that late and we haven't made love for quite a while.

SUE: Bob, don't take this personally, but I'm really not up for it tonight.

BOB: (turning on the light and sitting up in bed) Did I do something that turned you off?

SUE: No, don't be ridiculous. I love you, honey.

BOB: (sounding dismal) You sure don't act like it.

SUE: Bob, it's just that, well...

BOB: What are you trying to say? Just tell me.

SUE: It's sort of hard for me to put into words.

BOB: You're not attracted to me anymore. Is that it?

SUE: I swear that's not it. It's just that I feel sometimes like I'm on a merry-go-round that never seems to stop. You know, the day-to-day stuff that has to get done and then it feels like there's no time or energy left over for anything else.

BOB: Like lovemaking, for instance?

SUE: Yes. It's not that I don't want to. I do but I just get sort of physically and emotionally depleted. Actually, it's probably much more emotional than anything else.

Though, there are so many different feelings that people experience, the one which is most universal, is that of being worn out. It is a feeling that everyone can identify with and yet one which has no discernable beginning. You are not able to look back and point to a particular incident or time period when this feeling started to happen. It is even difficult to really put into words exactly what the feelings are. Being worn out is more of an underlying, yet ever present, general sense. Nothing is terribly wrong; nothing is very right. But what is clear is that this languor is there and it leaves you with a feeling that something is missing. Can you really point to what is missing? Most likely not. As you talk about this subject with friends, everyone is in agreement that they share the same feeling, along with an uncertainty about how to resolve it. Perhaps you speculate as to what could make things better. As you scan the possibilities, you may believe that the ideas for improvement seem silly or insignificant. If only he would buy me flowers once in awhile to let me know he appreciates the effort I put in with the kids; if only she would thank me for the hard week I put in at work. If only, if only - the list could go on and on. It is almost like you are making a big deal over nothing. Do you really need flowers to know that you are cared about? Do you really expect to be acknowledged for your job?

Being worn out is the final product of a culmination of stresses. Many people think that stress is some event, major or minor, that can be pinpointed. Sometimes it is. Perhaps, someone in the family had an extended illness; or maybe there was a flood in the house. But stress can also be lots of little things that build up. Some people liken it to the Chinese water torture. Each little incident is insignificant in and of itself. But little by little, it starts to become draining. Stress, by definition, is anything that requires coping. The stressor does not necessarily have to be negative. For example, imagine when your first child is entering kindergarten - certainly a joyous milestone. However, have you purchased all the right clothes, how will you arrange to get your child to school because there is a conflict with when the baby wakes up, will you buy all the right school supplies? Aside from the practical issues of your child entering school, there are also the emotional ones - for your child, for you. The child feels excited as well as apprehensive. You must deal with these issues. Your own feelings include happiness tinged with melancholy that your first child is leaving the nest and going off to school. You try to talk to your spouse about all of this but there really is not enough time, which also creates strain and stress. This situation serves as an example of one of many kinds of family business that are a natural part of life. Nothing serious is happening; yet, there are always circumstances requiring attention. Your family may well be at a different life cycle and so the particulars may vary. However, what remains constant are the small, non-critical situations that become day-to-day routines. Individually, they are manageable and mean nothing. But if they are put together, you are left with constantly having to deal with more than you can handle by yourself.

Obviously, there is a need to prioritize. Everything cannot be dealt with; the more important matters must come first. What often drops out first, and unfortunately fast, are the niceties. Things like noticing and appreciating each other go by the wayside and we start to take one another for granted. In one way, this is positive. We trust one another and presume there are good intentions. They do not always have to be recognized and reinforced. But at a certain point, the relationship suffers because no attention has really been paid to it. Too much has dropped off. So, we are left with a daily routine of little stresses and not any sense of appreciation. A dismal situation that leaves us feeling worn out comes to be the norm. Suddenly, the thought "there's got to be more than this" becomes a common one. Over time, without our knowing, the relationship has become one that is not bad, but far from good.

Do you leave such a marriage? No! The family still provides, among other things, security, safety, and a sense of joy. That is exactly why you have stayed. But, as of yet, you did not know how you got here, let alone how to make things better. Additionally, part of being worn out includes the sense that you have no time or energy to make things better. After all, there is still the homework, the laundry, the bill paying. The list goes on and on. The first thing necessary in order to relieve the worn out feeling is to decide to make your relationship important. Though at first glance, such an idea may seem frivolous, it is really a necessity. Devoting time to the relationship has important benefits to you, to your spouse, and to your family.

Worn Out Exercises:

3.   Everyone has their "to do" list. Do the following:

3a. On a piece of paper first list the tasks you feel must be accomplished in a given week.

3b. Now go back over that list and give each task a priority level which could be a system of 1-3. A #1 task is absolutely critical, a #2 task is important, and a #3 task would be great to get done but could wait if necessary.

3c.   Next to each task also determine if you are the only person to get these tasks done or is it possible to delegate on occasion, and write a "D" next to these items.

3d.   Once this prioritization is completed, go back and take all your #1 (critical tasks) and assign <u>how much time</u> you estimate they'll require (give it your best guess).

3e.   Now go to your weekly calendar and enter in your #1 (critical) tasks with their corresponding time allocations. Be sure that at least one of your <u>absolutely criticals</u> involves doing something <u>fun</u> with your mate.

3f.   Add to your list of #1 critical items, an allotment of "take care of me" time to be used however you wish. This may be only 15 minutes but try to build it in <u>every day</u> as part of your #1 priority list. Another option for some of you is to build in fewer activities that last longer (e.g. a 1-hour massage and 1-hour book club meeting for the week).

This is part of taking care of yourself and diminishing that worn out feeling.

3g.   Once you have gotten through your #1 critical tasks, if you have additional time you can add in your #2 important tasks, and so on, ultimately getting to your # 3 tasks.

3h.   After trying this exercise for a few weeks, discuss this strategy with your mate to see if (s)he may be interested in helping with some of the tasks you marked as "D" for delegate. You may also want to work on this exercise jointly to help one another out.

3i.   Once you work on this jointly, it's important to build in the same strategy of including "take care of us" time in addition to "take care of me" time. As an example, this "take care of us" time could be as simple as watching TV together or sharing an activity you both enjoy, as long as you make a conscious effort to spend time together.

FOUR

HOPELESS

Scenario 4

It's Friday night and Sue has come home a little early to prepare Bob's favorite meal as a gesture of trying to make amends because they've been having some ongoing bickering lately.

BOB: (walking into the house) Hi, Sue, something sure smells good!

SUE: I wanted to surprise you so I made your favorite dish, lasagna.

BOB: What's the special treatment for?

SUE: Just wanted to say "I love you" and I'm sorry about the fights we've had lately about our issues with your family.

BOB: Well, I'm sure I contributed to some of our arguments as well. By the way, I spoke to my mother today and they want to come visit over the holidays.

SUE: Oh. Did you tell her you wanted to double check with me, first?

BOB: Well, more or less. We didn't make definite plans.

SUE: Did you at least get around to the length of their stay, if they do come?

BOB: I'm sure it'll work out okay, trust me.

SUE: This isn't a trust thing.

BOB: Then what is it? Am I in the doghouse again?

SUE: Bob, it's about communication. We've been over this time and time again. You know how I feel about your parents visiting, plus the fact you never set limits with them and it's very intrusive having them here indefinitely.

BOB: What happened to being sweet with me and making my favorite dinner?

SUE: What happened to listening to each other and honoring each other's needs?

BOB: Damn it, Sue. You just can't let anything go anymore. Why does this have to turn into another fight? I'm too drained from my day to even deal with this right now.

SUE: Fine, Bob. I'm pretty tired too of our lack of communication. I don't know what to do next.

Perhaps, when it comes to understanding how relationships work, you consider yourself a bit more savvy than others. You are not among all those others who believed that love would be the answer to all your problems. You knew right from the start that in order for you and your mate to create harmony, there would have to be some effort; that it was not enough to just proclaim you were in love or just put in your time. Others of you may have initially hoped that when you and your spouse decided to create a partnership, it was because you believed that the two of you had more in common to make a relationship harmonious than you would with any other person. By virtue of this fact, you did expect things to be a bit easier. Now, you have come to realize that in order for the two of you to stay committed in a satisfying relationship, you need to put forth a conscious concern and extra effort.

Toward that end, you have tried a multitude of "tricks." You have tried letting your partner know when you are upset. Even making your spouse aware that you are not happy has been done in a number of ways - calmly, explaining, in anger, in writing. When you are aware of a problem, you have offered any number of suggestions from talking it out to seeking professional help. For some of you, getting the advice of a professional has actually been attempted. Sometimes in a sense of frustration, you became nasty or did not talk at all; at other times, you attempted to let the issue go and did your best to act nicely instead.

It seems that you have tried everything that there is to try. But it does not seem that anything is helping. Maybe, there is a momentary relaxation of tension. You attempt to forget about the squabble this morning about why he always runs at least an hour late and does not bother to call. Instead, you fix a lovely dinner and enjoy your meal together. Next week, he again neglects to let you know he is coming home late! You feel like she does not stop harping about the "stupid" thing your mother did; in your mind, the same point is made ad nauseam. But when you come home, you bring flowers. She is delighted; you are relieved. Relieved, that is, until you both sit down to watch TV together and she again brings up the mother subject!

Surely, all your efforts start to feel like they are in vain and a sense of hopelessness sets in. You are not even sure why you are reading this book. Only to try again with little hope that things can be different. Only to try again and be disappointed again. The sense of hopelessness is not a new feeling. In fact, it is a feeling that has become all too familiar to you and has started to become more a feeling of resignation. It is a lousy feeling but one it seems you have no choice but to start to accept.

Hopeless Exercises:

4a. Accept responsibility that you can change yourself and that usually, as you change, others will respond differently to you. So it is with your mate, in that as you begin to behave in new ways towards him or her, (s)he will typically begin to alter his or her behavior towards you as well.

4b. Remember things from your past that took a while to learn but now are so easy to do (riding a bike, driving, playing tennis, repairing a car). So it is with your relationship as well, and being patient is essential while you are trying new behaviors.

4c. Compliment yourself on your past attempts. Acknowledge that whatever you have tried in the past was done to the best of your ability, given what you knew. You definitely deserve credit for your efforts, regardless of how things turned out.

4d. Be willing to learn new ideas or handle things in a different way. You have nothing to lose except that nagging feeling of hopelessness.

4e. The very act of making a decision to change your own behavior is a significant choice. When we realize we have choices and then act on them, the result is generally feeling less hopeless.

FIVE

HURT

Scenario 5

As we rejoin Bob and Sue, they have both come home from work and are catching up on the events of the day. Sue decides to follow up on a home repair situation she's been dealing with.

SUE: ...So I assured my boss not to worry, I'd have the report finished by next Tuesday.

BOB: Good for you. Anything else goin' on?

SUE: Well, I'm still dealing with the problem we're having with our furnace and you can't believe what a headache it's turned into.

BOB: What's the big deal? Can't they just come out and fix the darn thing?

SUE: Well, that's what I thought, but I keep getting transferred to

different people each time I call and I've had no luck with customer

service, either.

BOB: Well, it sounds like it's time for me to step in and get involved. Fill

me in on the details and I'll handle it.

SUE: What does that mean?

BOB: Just what I said. It's no big deal.

SUE: Maybe it's not a big deal to you. But trust me, I have it under

control.

BOB: I know you can handle it.

SUE: That's not what it sounded like to me!

BOB: What're you talking about? Why are you so sensitive all the time?

SUE: Oh, so now it's my fault for being insensitive. For the third time

this week you imply I'm incompetent - and the problem is "I'm

sensitive!"

BOB: Jeez, this is ridiculous. I've had it. (He leaves the room angrily.)

A common feeling that many of us experience is that of hurt. We

know we feel it and yet, it is hard to describe. It is more like a vague

unpleasant sensation. Though feeling hurt is not gender specific, it is probably more recognizable to women. It occurs when your spouse forgets to inquire about the important doctor's appointment you had. Not making a big enough deal about a promotion would certainly lead to a sense of hurt. Missed anniversaries or birthdays are likely to result in a person feeling hurt. Clearly, all these examples could apply to either a male or a female. So, it is the recognition of the hurt, not the experiencing of it, which women do more easily.

Usually, people have a vague sense that something feels uncomfortable. They may feel that they have been slighted in some way. It seems as if the mate is not concerned enough. Or, they can more readily express that they feel that their feelings do not matter. The bottom line is often that the wounded party feels that she or he does not matter all that much to the mate.

If hurt feelings could be easily expressed and understood, residual problems would not ensue. Speaking stereotypically, a woman will more likely let her mate know she is hurt. However, often, a male is not equipped to offer a woman a response that is satisfying to her. This then leads to an additional hurt reaction on the part of the woman. When a man gets hurt, more likely than not, he does not readily notice it or does not express it. In either case, the hurt does not get addressed. Typical of all emotions, when hurt is not attended to it does not go away on its own. Rather, the feeling lies dormant, acting as a potential trigger for other emotions. It has been my experience in working with couples that anger is often the product of unexpressed hurt that has built up over time. As painful as hurt is, it is easier to deal with than anger. Once anger sets in, it is likely that each person in the relationship has become somewhat hardened and may be less receptive to communicating his or her issues or listening to what each other has to say.

Hurt Exercises:

5a. When you experience feeling hurt, it may help to try and clarify some of your feelings on paper. Start by comparing your responses to the following questions: "What did I expect my mate to do or say in this particular situation?;" "What did my mate actually do or say in this particular situation?" As you review your responses try to identify where the **gap** occurred.

5b. Once you have clarified on paper, and in your mind, where the gap is between what you *expected* your mate to do or say, and what (s)he *actually did*, you have the option of sharing this with your partner. Make sure to do so by talking about your feelings rather than attacking what (s)he did or did not do. Remember to focus on the WHAT, and not the WHO. Emphasis is on the behavior, rather than on the person. As an example, you could say: "Although it wasn't intentional, I felt hurt when you didn't ask me about my physical exam, because I feel like I'm not important to you." (Further clarification on expressing your feelings can be found in the Communication Skills section.)

5c. Once you have shared your hurt feelings with your mate, (s)he may offer an apology to you. Be understanding and forgiving when your partner has done something that is not perfect. Let them know you still love them for who they are. As an example, you could say: "I appreciate that you listened to me and understand why I feel hurt and this doesn't change how I feel about you."

5d. When you share your hurt feelings with your mate, (s)he may also open up and reveal that they too feel hurt by a behavior you exhibited. Listen openly to what they say and then take ownership for your behavior and offer a sincere apology to your mate. As an example, you could say: "I didn't realize I hurt your feelings and certainly didn't intend to do that. I'm sorry for my behavior. Please know that I love you."

SIX

APPREHENSION

Scenario 6

Bob is out of town for the weekend on a combination business/pleasure trip and Sue finds she has a little extra time on her hands. She decides to phone her girlfriend Carol and do some catching up.

SUE: Hi, Carol, guess who? Got a few extra minutes to gab with an old friend?

CAROL: I'm so glad you called. I've been looking for a good excuse to take a break from the millions of chores I have piled up for the day. How's it goin'?

SUE: Oh you know, same old, same old, I suppose.

CAROL: You sound a little out of sorts. Things okay with you and Bob?

SUE: Sure, we get along and everything. Well, you know how we are as a couple, right?

CAROL: Look, Sue, no couple has a marriage made in heaven and I know you two have your ups and downs. It's not that different in my relationship, either.

SUE: Yeah, I know what you mean but there are times when I just wish we had what other couples seem to have...or for that matter what we used to have before life got so complicated.

CAROL: I remember last time when we talked about this, you were going to start to take a few steps; try some different things. Did anything come of that?

SUE: Well, I did start to pursue some things. I think I've read just about every self-help book out there, clipped out some great tips from some of my magazines and have spent some time looking at some pretty good websites for couples.

CAROL: I can relate. I've found myself doing similar things. Hey, remember I gave you the name of a colleague of mine who is a counselor specializing in relationships? Ever call her?

SUE: Not only did I call her, we had a few appointments. She seemed to know her stuff.

CAROL: So you feel like you've done it all?

SUE: That's right. I could probably be an expert with all I know. Now all I need to figure out is what to do about my own relationship, now that I have all this valuable input.

CAROL: So what's holding you back? Any clues?

SUE: I guess I'm so afraid of what will happen if I try to do things differently with Bob. Even something simple like wanting to spend more time together which would mean he'd spend less time with the guys playing golf, watching sports, surfing the Internet.

CAROL: Think that'd be a problem for him?

SUE: I don't know; maybe, maybe not. What if he reacts negatively and gives me a hard time? Or what if he was willing to change and then we found we didn't really enjoy more time together? Maybe we just don't have what I think we have and I'm opening up a real can of worms here.

CAROL: So where would that leave you if that were the case?

SUE: You mean if Bob and I...

CAROL: Yes. If you and Bob weren't right for each other.

SUE: I can't even imagine what starting over would be like. What a

          nightmare.

CAROL: I think you're jumping the gun. Why not start at the beginning

          and let him know how you feel and see how he feels? You two

          sound a little out of touch.

SUE: You really think I can do it?

CAROL: I'm pulling for you, Sue. Why just keep doing the same old

          routine?

Whether you did not have any unrealistic expectations from the beginning or whether you have come to accept the idea that a relationship requires work is not important. The fact is that you do agree that relationships need work and you are open to such work in your own marriage. You are aware of all the resources that are out there to help you - therapists, self-help books, chat rooms, magazine articles - to name a few. You do not let your pride stand in the way of referring to some of these resources and it's probably a good idea to talk it through with a close friend. After all, no marriage is perfect, right?

Yet, with all these good intentions, you still feel that sort of queasy uneasiness. The feeling of uneasiness is apparent because with all of the information you have at your disposal, you still do nothing. There are lots of reasons why no action is taken - you are tired, or you forgot, or you'll start to deal with these concerns after the holidays, or... While the reasons may be endless, they are in actuality, excuses for not confronting issues in your relationship. Excuses are sometimes the result of feeling apprehensive. If this is something that is happening to you, it is probably *apprehension* you are experiencing, much the same way that Sue felt about speaking to Bob regarding changing the routine in their marriage.

Apprehension, by definition, is a fear of what *might* be coming. For some, this is tied into a discomfort with change. After all, change implies something new and/or different. New and different means something that is unknown and, therefore, out of one's control. As an example, let's say your mate is always the one to make the social arrangements. Perhaps this makes you uncomfortable - you want to be the one to make those plans occasionally. Or, maybe your mate makes the plans but often does so at the last minute and opportunities are lost. Well, certainly a good way to do something different would be for you to make the plans. Though it sounds like a great idea and certainly one that is simple enough, you hesitate in following through. There it is - that nagging sense of apprehension. What if your mate feels your initiative indicated a sense of disapproval of how they were doing it? What if your plan interferes with a surprise plan made by your partner? What if your plan isn't PERFECT?

Though these concerns are meaningful, there is another form of apprehension that is more crippling. Many of you, like Sue, are not sure how the other person feels. You worry about whether it is too late to get this relationship to function in a satisfying way or even be saved. This can be an overwhelming notion, and you don't want to face this head on... or do you? The thought of making efforts only to have them rejected seems much too scary. It feels safer to allow things to stay as they are than to place yourself in a vulnerable position. Vulnerable can be equated with taking a risk, and sometimes you're not ready to, as Robert Frost suggested, "take the road less traveled." But, what if you did? It could very well make "all the difference!"

Apprehension Exercises:

6a. Be aware of the concept that if you keep doing something the same way, things will remain as they are. If you want something to have a different outcome, you have to do something in a way that you haven't tried before.

Write down the ingredients for your favorite dessert recipe. Now imagine that you have a friend coming for dinner who has dietary restrictions and cannot consume sugar. What would you do in order to accommodate your friend (e.g. use a substitute ingredient, leave the ingredient out or choose a different dessert)? Challenge yourself to see how many alternatives you can come up with to handle this situation. This will be good practice to break away from always doing something the same way.

Now think about the benefits of doing something in a different way (e.g. in this case changing the recipe), and make a note of them.

6b. Be honest with yourself. Think about the aspects in your relationship that you find unsatisfying. Make a list putting the dissatisfying areas in order from the least to the most difficult to confront or think about.

Starting with the first item on your list (least difficult to confront), focus on the following: "What would need to change in order for you to feel satisfied?," "What would need to happen in order to achieve this result?," and "What steps can you take to act differently toward your partner so your goal can be accomplished?" Write your answers down so you can review them and make any necessary changes.

6c. As you reflect on what has to happen, spend time thinking about how to approach your partner. This is someone you have been with for a while and you know a lot about him or her. In your imagination, try out various scenarios; you'll be able to tell which ones are the better ones as you let yourself explore the possibilities (e.g. talking over dinner, going out for a walk and talking, etc.). Remember to think about how you say things (e.g. "I want to share some thoughts with you about keeping our relationship strong," or "It's important to me that we work on making our relationship the best it can be, so can we spend some time talking?"). Try saying some of these statements aloud; how do they sound (for those of you looking for additional feedback, you may also talk in front of a mirror while tape recording yourself)? Intonation, gestures, and body language all impact what you say. Make sure you emphasize *your* perceptions or experiences and are careful not to attack your partner. Take a risk, remembering that to *get* a change you have to *make* one.

SEVEN

MISUNDERSTOOD

Scenario 7

It is the weekend and Sue has been out running errands for several hours and now comes home to Bob who is reading the newspaper, but seems distracted.

SUE: Bob, I'm back. (No response from Bob)

SUE: Bob, did you hear me? I said I'm home and could use some help putting things away.

BOB: (sounding somewhat dismal) Oh, okay, sure. Can I get to it a little later?

SUE: Later? You don't look all that busy now, Bob. What's the problem?

BOB: I don't know. Just feel like doing it later, like I said.

SUE: (frustrated) Fine! Any calls while I was out?

BOB: Yeah, my dad called.

SUE: Oh...how'd that go?

BOB:(sounding depressed) Pretty much the usual. You know how we have our issues and I dread his calls because he and I just don't relate.

SUE: Right. Well, here's what I think needs to happen. You two need to have a heart-to-heart talk, put the issues out on the table and...

BOB: (cutting her off) Sue, this is the last thing I want to discuss, right now.

SUE: But, I was just trying to help. I thought you wanted that.

BOB: Well, you thought wrong. What I need is to be left alone right now.

When you were first dating your mate, not only did everything feel wonderful, you felt like you had finally met someone who understood you. That person listened and could grasp what you meant. Finally there was someone with whom you didn't have to spell everything out. Sometimes, a "look" was all that was needed. You would come out of a movie theater and go for coffee. As you shared your reactions to the movie, the person at the other end of the table smiled knowingly or nodded his/her head. You would leave a party and on the ride home, share stories about the evening. Without much explanation, (s)he "got it." It was so nice to be involved with someone who understood you.

As you look back on these memories, you may wonder, "What ever happened to that person I knew? How come I feel so misunderstood now?" You relate an incident that happened at work but are met with a blank look. Someone acted outrageously in the parking lot; but when you tell your mate the story, (s)he seems to take the other person's side. You try directly, and appropriately, to tell your spouse how you feel you need more help around the house. The answer (s)he offers, that you be less compulsive, is non-responsive to your point. And an argument quickly escalates as you try unsuccessfully to have your point understood. Communication starts to become very frustrating.

As upsetting as all this may be, feeling heard and understood again is quite possible. The main difference between when you were dating and now is one of a priority factor. When you were first going out with each other, the two of you each held the other's views as a top priority. Part of the reason for this is was, because, at that time in your lives, forming a relationship was the priority. As you live this part of your life, other issues have taken center stage, mostly your family. Though reprioritizing in this way is appropriate, it leaves less time for the two of you. Over and above a pure time factor, family needs interfere with the ability to communicate in satisfying ways. Because there is so much going on, you cannot be totally available in a clear manner to your partner. Also, much of what does go on in your daily life has some emotional "charge" which gets in the way of clear communication. The result is that neither you nor your partner has the time or patience to really listen to the other.

Misunderstood Exercises:

7a. Suggest to your mate that the two of you set aside time each day, or several times a week, for the two of you to talk privately and "catch up" with one another. When you have something you want to talk about, plan to do so during this designated time. However, if you feel what you need to discuss <u>can't</u> wait, then make this known to your mate as well, and ask when there might be some available time sooner than what was planned or request that your mate make this a priority. As an example, you could say: "I know we have our 'catch up' time later tonight, but I'm feeling pretty bad right now and would really appreciate it if you could make some time for me now."

7b. If your mate starts to talk to you and you are preoccupied with something else, indicate that you cannot really pay attention right now, but suggest an alternate time that would work well and see if it also works for your mate. As an example, you could say: "I'm really interested in hearing your thoughts, however I'm right in the middle of reading an article for work. Is it okay with you if we have this conversation in a half-hour?" However, if your mate doesn't readily agree and feels (s)he wants to speak *now*, you may need to reprioritize your plans to be more accommodating, as stated in #7a above. It's especially important to reciprocate if your mate has done the same for you.

7c. When you are in the middle of a conversation with your mate and perceive that you're being misunderstood, you may want to try to communicate this directly rather than jump to erroneous conclusions. Try to use an "I message" to let your mate know what you're feeling at the moment, and then let him or her respond to you. This is one way of checking your perceptions. As an example, you can say: "I'd like to stop for a moment and let you know how I'm feeling. I feel that I just shared a lot of frustration with you about my day and I'm upset because I get the sense that you feel I'm making a mountain out of a mole hill." (For further explanation of an "I message" refer to the Communication Skills section.)

EIGHT

UNAPPRECIATED

Scenario 8

Bob and Sue have just sat down to dinner and are catching up on what's been going on for both of them.

BOB: Hey, Sue, did I mention that I'll need to head out of town this

　　　weekend for a special training seminar that just came up?

SUE: Oh, you're kidding! That's in a couple of days, you know. It's such

　　　last minute notice.

BOB: Tell me about it. But I just found out about it myself. Believe me,

　　　I'm not looking forward to it, given how hectic things are in the

　　　office right now.

SUE: Hectic in the office, what about at home or haven't you noticed?

BOB: I know we have the usual craziness; is that what you mean?

SUE: The "usual" craziness? Just this week alone, I've had to leave work early twice to deal with the kids' school events, and a new carpooling schedule. And did you forget this weekend you were supposed to go the soccer game so I could get my rescheduled haircut appointment in?

BOB: Oops. Yeah, I completely forgot about that one.

SUE: The thing is, it's not the first time this has happened.

BOB: (With a tinge of anger) I know, but come on, you know I'm up for this promotion and I have to pay my dues. I'm doing this for us. I thought you understood that!

SUE: That's not the point at all. I just don't think you realize how much I do to keep things going in this family and what do I get as a reward? I have to miss my hair appointment so I can be at the kids' game since you have yet another commitment! When will this end?

You consider yourself to be a grown-up who has taken on the responsibility of being in a committed relationship. You accept the fact that responsibilities are part of this commitment. These responsibilities include household chores, tasks that help the family run smoothly, attending to the children and their needs, giving your spouse some extra help when necessary, responding to unpredicted small emergencies, and reprioritizing for unexpected major life events. The list can go on and on. You have accepted this lifestyle and generally deal with it pretty well.

But what about you? How often do you have to put your wants and needs on hold? After a particularly harried day, you fall into the easy chair and actually let yourself rest - but only for 15 minutes. As you close your eyes, your mind races. And then, all of a sudden, a thought hits you! It's not that you actually mind doing all that you do; what really bothers you is the fact that none of your efforts ever seem to be appreciated. No one ever says "thank you" for the chores you have done. No one notices that the dirty clothes have been picked up off the floor, laundered, folded, and put back into drawers. Do they think a fairy came along and did all that work? As you are taking out the garbage (surely another unnoticed task), you realize that one of the tires on the car looks low. Without saying anything, you go to the gas station to put in air. While driving there, you realize the fuel tank indicator is on "E." Of course, you fill the car with gas. All part of running a family, but did the other members think those things got attended to magically? You drive yet one more family member somewhere. "Here we are," you joyfully say and the person responds back, "Bye." But where was the "thank you?" Even a taxicab driver would be thanked - it's common courtesy.

When spouses start to feel unappreciated, it often leads to a sense of being used. Not only is this a negative feeling but it can also create other residual negative emotions and behaviors (e.g. talking back abruptly). It is difficult to continue acting in a positive way, if, when you do, you feel unappreciated. It starts to feel like, "what you do does not matter anyway, so why do it?"

Unappreciated Exercises:

Perhaps the best way to show someone they are appreciated is to go out of your way (even if only slightly) to do something nice for them. For example:

8a. An old, but consistently appreciated behavior is that of buying flowers. What is not so customary is a woman buying them for a man. But men do, in fact, appreciate receiving flowers/plants. So, not only will they be valued by a woman receiving them but also by the man getting them from his mate. If flowers seem a bit costly, one flower is as meaningful because, in reality, it is the thought that matters and not the flower, per se. Along the same line, with a slightly different twist is to send balloons. How silly, how much fun, how appreciated!

8b. Perhaps you are always considerate and let your mate know that (s)he is thought of when Hallmark has created special dates - birthdays, anniversaries, Valentine's Day. It is not in any way being suggested that those gestures should be given up. But an unexpected card, whether it be romantic or silly, lets the other person know they are appreciated.

8c. In this day of technology, there are other options available to us. Make a call to your partner for no reason other than to say, "Hi." Or, make the call when you know your partner is not around. Receiving a nice sentiment through a message really means a great deal. For those of you who are even more technologically advanced, send an e-mail.

8d. Have you gone out to run one of the endless carpools? Make a quick stop and surprise your mate with a favorite dessert, or just some treat that is special to them that they may not get for themselves (not recommended for partners who are trying to watch their weight).

8e. Acts of kindness do not have to cost money. Some of the nicest things you can do for your partner are acts of service. Such things as doing the laundry, letting him know a TV show he would be interested in is going to be on, taking out the garbage, or getting home early so your partner can get to an event she is interested in, all count favorably. Labors that take minor effort become acts of appreciation and love. Also remember that saying, "Thank you for doing the shopping" (or whatever chore your mate typically does) and what effect this had on you (like, "This saved me so much time"). A comment like this is music to someone's ears and lets them know their efforts are not taken for granted. You can also offer to do your mate's chores for the day so they feel like they got a break and can do something they want to do.

8f. So, your day got away from you and you forgot to do any of these things. Not to worry. Let your partner know that while at lunch or driving somewhere they were in your thoughts. There is no doubt that hearing this will make your partner feel good.

NINE

NEGLECTED

Scenario 9

As we look in on Sue and Bob at this time, Sue has recently been asked to take on additional responsibilities at work and has just been named the head of her department. She is both excited and anxious about this new development and seems very focused on proving herself. She has just called Bob to tell him she'll be home late.

SUE: Hi, honey. Bad news, I can't make it home in time for dinner tonight.

BOB: What's going on?

SUE: Oh you know how it goes at this office. Now that I have this new title, my day knows no end. Guess you'll have to pull dinner together for everyone and help the kids with their homework.

BOB: Well, you won't be home that late, will you? There's a great game

on tonight that I want to watch.

SUE: Really can't say. Gotta' go.

(Several hours later, Sue arrives home.)

BOB: Thank goodness you're finally home. I've had a heck of a night

and that's not even considering what my day was like.

SUE: Well, I'm exhausted but I have some loose ends to finish up on the

computer.

BOB: You're doing more work now! It's 10:30 at night.

SUE: The supervisor's job is never done. You understand, right?

BOB: Do I have a choice? How about spending 5 minutes with your old

man?

SUE: Wish I could, honey. Maybe tomorrow night, okay?

You are committed to your family. Your spouse is a good and decent

person who, like you, takes the relationship and family responsibilities

seriously. Also, like you, your lifetime partner is overwhelmed and tired.

There is a lot to take care of if a family is to be run properly. Prioritizing

is a necessity. Though you understand and comprehend all of these

concepts logically, there are times when the needs and emotions you have beg to be addressed. You do not want to run the carpool. You do not want to walk the dog. You do not want to help with math problems. What you *do* want to do is to read the newspaper for once.

There is a gnawing feeling that starts to be ever present. Day after day, week after week, something or someone is always coming before you. You lose your personal sense of "space." Even worse, you no longer have your own identity. You start to be known as somebody's mother or father. Perhaps, you start to feel like you're nothing more than hired help. Maybe images of you being nothing more than a "meal ticket," chauffeur, or maid start to invade your thought processes. There may be times you envision screaming, "What about me? Don't I count?"

The sense of having your needs not being fulfilled often surfaces regardless of children. Your favorite entertainer will be in concert in your hometown. Is it too much to expect that your mate would accompany you with a good attitude? Or, is it too much to expect that he would come even with a not so good attitude? You have just come out of a very busy season at work. You two have been invited to a party at the house of a family member. Why is she not able to understand that you would rather pass this one time and be willing to go by herself? After all, this is her family, not a bunch of strangers. Your spouse has had several situations come up, one after another, which have truly deserved attention. As a grown-up and concerned partner, you have put your needs aside to be available without resenting it. But would it be too much to hope for a greeting when you walk in the door? You make a request of your spouse to take care of something for you that is important but that you cannot get to; he agrees to take care of it for you. "Great," you think; but then it never gets done.

None of these examples is catastrophic. Any one of them can easily be overlooked. But when small things start to build up, they create a cumulative effect. Often, the result is that one or both of you feel unimportant, neglected, and/or disregarded.

Neglected Exercises:

9a. Say nice things to each other. Compliment your partner on how they look before they leave for the day or just after getting a haircut or makeover. This shows you're paying attention to them and are attracted to them.

9b. Go on a date with your partner. Being short on funds or time does not have to interfere. It is not necessary to leave the premises to feel like you are on a date. All you have to do is rent a video and pop some popcorn. The real trick is to stay committed to your plan. Make sure the kids have gone to bed. Turn down the lights, put the VCR on, put your feet up (a definite advantage of an at-home date) and enjoy both the movie and your time together. Not all your home dates have to be movie watching. There's lots of room for creativity.

9c. "Steal" a half-hour together. Of course, you could be doing 100 other important things. But you and your partner are of the utmost importance. A short walk or drive together for no purpose but to relax and spend some time together goes a long way.

9d. Somewhere in the closet, there are some old photographs. It does not matter if they are loose or set up in an album. Take them out to look at together. Enjoy the memories and re-ignite some of the old sparks.

9e. Try to "surprise" or delight your partner with something special for them. Maybe have their favorite dinner waiting for them when they come home and share the meal with some candlelight. Or pack up a quick picnic lunch and show up at your spouse's job and steal them away for a quick bite together.

TEN

BORED

Scenario 10

BOB: Boy am I glad tomorrow's Friday!

SUE: Yeah, me too. It sure has been one helluva work week.

BOB: You know what? I think this is the first weekend in months we've both had completely free.

SUE: Wow! You're right! My calendar is open for both Saturday and Sunday.

BOB: Mine too. Amazing. So, what should we do this weekend?

SUE: I don't know, what did you have in mind?

BOB: I'm not sure. Guess I was hoping you had an idea. Let's see if we can think of something really fun.

SUE: Hmmm. Let me see...nothing's jumping out right now.

BOB: How about dinner and a movie?

SUE: C'mon, we always do that. Besides, there isn't a single movie out

we both want to see.

BOB: Okay. What about going to that annual antique car show we used

to go to?

SUE: Nah. It's such a long drive, and frankly, it's a lot more fun for you

than it is for me. What about the crafts fair?

BOB: Not interested. We just walk around and around and never agree

on what to buy. Where's the fun in that?

SUE: Where's the fun in anything we do together anymore?

BOB: I hate to admit it, but it seems we each have a better time when

we go our separate ways.

SUE: What happened to us, Bob? We used to love doing everything

together.

It is not that you have nothing to do. Your days are busy and often,

you find yourself hurrying along in order to get everything done that you

need to complete. At the end of a day, and certainly by the end of the

week, you are tired. Your week has been filled with work, house

cleaning, doing the laundry, helping the kids with homework, running

household chores. Yet, underneath the tiredness there is something else gnawing at you. Well, perhaps you need to rest a bit. So, you actually take the luxury of a nap. The half hour "mini-vacation" is nice, but when you get up, the same sensation is still there. Was it something you forgot to do? Quickly, you run through the family "necessities." No, that is not it. And, then, it hits you. As strange as it may seem with all that is going on, you are bored!

Many people associate boredom with having nothing to do; they feel the need to have some kind of stimulating situation. But boredom can also come about in spite of having a great deal to do. It can be the result of tedium. Though there is something happening, it is the same old thing. Humans, being a highly developed species, require intellectual stimulation. Though the degree of complexity or the rate of frequency may differ from person to person, some variation is necessary for each of us. This need is so vital that if we do not have it, our initial development as a child may be thwarted. In later years, deprivation from new kinds of stimulation can create a real hardship to our mental well-being. When we do the same thing, repeatedly, the task becomes mindless. By mindless I mean that we do not have to think about it. The constant repetition of the behavior helps it to become a habit, something that can be done by rote. Habitual behavior does offer us something positive because we do not have to think about every little thing. We can, therefore, have the ability to devote ourselves to more challenging tasks. But if our life starts to become nothing more than repetitious behaviors, it leads to a sense of being uninteresting, tedious, and tiring. Though it may feel like the amount of activity level is what's making you tired, actually, it is the humdrum of it which is the cause.

Within a relationship, each partner individually has experiences that provide satisfaction to a greater or lesser extent - career, friends, hobbies. But when it comes to the relationship as an entity, if you're experiencing a sense of boredom, there's a good chance that your partner is feeling similarly. Your partner may very well be in the same humdrum rut as you or, your boredom may have contagiously spread to your partner. If it reaches this level, the ramifications are far more damaging and even thinking about working on the relationship may seem like a Herculean effort.

Being a responsible family member, you may think that it is irresponsible to take time for yourself. Or, it may feel frivolous to you to expect to engage in activities that seem to serve no purpose other than to have fun. But fun is not only fun; it helps to recharge us so that we can continue with our responsibilities. Most of us have heard the concept that vacations are important because they refuel us. For some, luxurious restful vacations are not really an option. Budgets or parental responsibilities may restrict taking advantage of a vacation. Others may be more fortunate. But from my work with couples, I rarely see, certainly on any kind of regular basis, the refueling spontaneity that is necessary to keep a relationship vibrant. In order for a partnership to keep from becoming a habit, and a stale one at that, it is vitally important that the boredom factor be addressed.

Bored Exercises:

10a. Be willing to do something out of the ordinary, something that you do not usually do. It does not have to be something outrageous or costly - just different. The difference from the routine is what makes it enjoyable. As an example, it can be as simple as renting a video you've been dying to see, going out to a special sale event or making time to meet a friend with whom you've been out of touch. (Notice that this exercise is being suggested for you to do on your own. Not everything to improve a relationship has to be something that involves both of you. Remember that when one person makes a change, it is likely to have an impact on the other person, and therefore, the relationship. Also, by doing some things on your own, it allows you to have experiences to share with your partner.)

10b. Participate in an activity that usually your partner does without you. Go into it with an open mind rather than a sense that you won't like it. As an example, try out a sport with your mate like golfing or tennis.

10c. Exchange the usual responsibilities you each do. This helps prevent boredom and also enhances an understanding of what your partner experiences.

10d. Create some surprise for the two of you to do together. Spontaneity is a wonderful antidote to boredom. As an example, sign the two of you up for a class or plan a "mystery drive" somewhere for the day.

10e. Laughter is not only the best medicine, it is a great cure for boredom. If you can, at least once a month go to a comedy club together. No comedy clubs in your city or town? Perhaps your local theater is running a comedic play! No theater? Then rent a comedy classic video such as The Marx Brothers or modern comedies featuring Steve Martin or Robin Williams.

ELEVEN

UNROMANTIC

Scenario 11

It's a weekday night and Sue is beginning to prepare dinner. Bob comes home unexpectedly early tonight which surprises Sue.

BOB: Hey, guess who's home?

SUE: This is a surprise! Is anything wrong?

BOB: Why does something have to be wrong if a man comes home a little early to see his beautiful wife?

SUE: You're awfully sweet, Bob. Now really, what're you up to?

BOB: (putting his arms around Sue's waist) You just have a suspicious mind and all I want to do is get in a little extra time with you, seeing as how our schedules have been so nutty.

SUE: Unfortunately, tonight's not much better. I need to get dinner going a

little early so I can get to the PTA meeting at the kids' school.

BOB: (turning on the stereo) Hey listen, our song's on the radio! May I

have this dance?

SUE: Who's got time to dance now? Look, it's almost 6:00; I'll never fit

everything in that needs to get done!

BOB: So, you're a few minutes late for the PTA, who's gonna notice?

You have a good excuse - tell them you couldn't resist your

husband.

SUE: Bob, this just isn't the best time. Maybe after this weekend, okay?

BOB: (disappointed) You want me to put my feelings on hold till after

the weekend? What happened to the spontaneity in our lives?

SUE: I guess our lives have changed a lot.

Can you recall the good ol' days when you would take strolls together

arm-in-arm, nuzzle up to one another on the sofa or give each other a

quick peck on the cheek for no reason?

Now, you find it's hard to remember the last time you were romantic

with each other. The only romance in your life seems to be derived from

the movies you watch or the books you read. The stupid marriage jokes about the lack of sex are all too meaningful. These are common feelings experienced by people in long-term relationships.

The lack of a romantic component is often the result of connecting becoming a low priority. A million other things require your attention. The lack of time automatically impacts the romance. Additionally, as has been discussed previously, when relationship maintenance starts to take low priority, other negative feelings begin to surface and are likely to get in the way of wanting to act romantically.

Romance is a form of communication and it is the product of good communication. It requires being aware of your partner. Romance, may or may not involve sex. Rather, included are small gestures that offer signs of connection like holding hands, cuddling, or putting a caring arm around your partner. When romance and sex do occur together, it is lovemaking. There is certainly a place for more basic sex in a partnership, but sex continually without tenderness may lead to empty feelings for one or both people. Romance, on the other hand, has a broader scope for a relationship. It lets your partner know you care. So, even when times are hassled and the two of you are just too exhausted to be physically intimate, the connection is preserved.

Unromantic Exercises:

11a. Leave a note on the mirror with lipstick or by writing with the steamed-up mirror. (Obviously, the second is easier for clean up purposes and is simple, but private – and that's what makes it so appealing.)

11b. If your spouse "brown bags" his or her lunch, slip a private note inside the bag to tell them how much they mean to you.

11c. Give each other massages or back scratches. These can be done with clothes on or off and can take place either in bed or while watching TV. How the specifics are played out will depend on your comfort level. The goal here is not to necessarily be sensual leading to sex, but to start connecting on a more physical level.

11d. Bring some sensuous food that you can feed each other, to bed (e.g. grapes, strawberries, etc. and of course, whipped cream or chocolate syrup to dip them in). This is food you're going to play with, and tease each other with, as much as eat. As should be apparent by now, the specifics are left to you. Some of you will want to share a meal while watching TV or a video in bed. Others may want to concentrate just on the meal and having some quiet talk. (As you consider whether to do this with or without clothes, remember that eating in bed may get sloppy and so a cleaning bill may be the consequence.)

11e. When was the last time you danced together? For most of us, it has been at some official function like a wedding or dinner dance. But at those times, the dance is more an "appropriate" activity shared by many on the dance floor with you. Perhaps some of you have gotten into the recent ballroom craze. That's great but still not the point. Put on a slow song, perhaps one that has meaning for the two of you and enjoy each other's company. Enjoy that old feeling of being special and feeling tender. Recall the time when it seemed like you were the only two people in the world. A short dance of 4-5 minutes does a lot to re-create that feeling.

11f. Lots of research has indicated the benefit of physical touch. It creates a sense of closeness and intimacy. Physical touch in the form of affection (gentle touch or a tender kiss), says a great deal to your partner. Cuddling is especially rewarding: at night, it gives a sense of completeness to the day; in the morning, it seems to start everything off with a much better perspective.

11g. Pack a picnic lunch on the spur of the moment and bring along a cassette tape with some of your favorite music for setting the right atmosphere. Afterwards or before lunch, take a walk in the park and stop to spend some time on a swing or seesaw or perhaps sit and enjoy a sunset together.

11h. Make it a rule that each of you put forth at least one romantic effort each day, no matter how small, no matter the duration. Come up with a "penalty" (monetary or a chore) for each time you miss your daily romantic gesture.

TWELVE

RESENTMENT/ANGER

Scenario 12

It's a weekend morning and Bob and Sue are mapping out their plans.

SUE: So, what's on your agenda this weekend?

BOB: Well, if I luck out and the weather stays good, I'm definitely playing golf with the guys.

SUE: Not the whole day, I hope.

BOB: Can't say for sure. Guess I'll play it by ear.

SUE: Well, let's see if I can be more direct. I was hoping you'd get the yard work done and bring the car in for its maintenance work.

BOB: Why don't you throw in painting the house while you're at it!

SUE: I would but I know it can't get done in a weekend and the other two are the priorities.

BOB: You're some slave driver, you are!

SUE: Maybe that's because I could use a little help around here.

BOB: Did you ever think of asking me in a nice way?

SUE: I've been doing that but gave up when I didn't get results.

BOB: Funny, I don't remember hearing you use a different tone of voice.

SUE: Maybe that's because most of the time you've tuned me out.

BOB: Sounds like you have a laundry list of complaints.

SUE: I do all the juggling of everything around here and I'm so tired of having to keep at you to do your share.

BOB: I'm late for my golf game.

As we become more comfortable in our relationship, we feel safer. We are, therefore, willing to be more open. However, for most of us, being open also leaves us more vulnerable. The person with whom we initially felt safe enough to express ourselves now becomes the potential aggressor. She knows who and what we are; she knows our weak spots; she knows how to "get us." We might even become apprehensive about the other person's motives. Yet, what has changed is *not* the other person but *our* perception. Our perception is now distorted by a sense of vulnerability. The very same comment that you can laugh about when stated by a friend, is quite upsetting when made by your mate. For example, you tell your friend that you are thinking about taking dance lessons. Your friend retorts, "You must think you're a kid again!" You both laugh and the conversation goes on. You make this same remark to your mate, who gives you the same answer. Only when your mate says it, you hear the comment as a judgment - that you are too old and that there is something wrong with you. You become offended and further perceive that your mate does not understand you or your needs; perhaps, you think, your mate does not really care. Most of this goes on without you even knowing that it is happening. If you were aware that this dynamic was happening, you would, at least, have the choice of talking about it. For most of us, it just registers and is pushed down into that emotional "black hole." Or, maybe you were aware that something was bothering you but decided not to make a fuss. It would be nice if we could say that it was never to be heard from again. On the contrary, these little hurts build up and eventually "leak." Usually, the leak comes out as a low-level tension and a sense of uneasiness is experienced. Or, the resentment may manifest as an attack of your mate.

Attacks can come in many different forms but, in some way, are expressions of negativity to your mate. In many instances, vocal tones become very sharp or have "an edge" to them. In its blunt form, an attack includes name-calling - "you're such a jerk" or "what a bitch." At a more subtle level are statements like, "I can never count on you to help me when I need it" or "Can't you ever stop harping on the same issue?"

Attacks are not necessarily direct but also can be expressed in ways that minimize the other person. An example of this would be, "Why are you making such a big deal of this?" or "You never get my point." Vocal language does not have to be used to convey a negative message. Body language or facial expressions, like rolling one's eyes, can easily send out a message that lets your partner know you think what they are expressing is worthless or stupid. In a different version, though still one that is undermining, is when one partner raises an issue and the other hardly acknowledges it. This form comes out as either offering no response (stonewalling), or not paying attention at all. Lots of people think that if they just say nothing, they have no responsibility in escalating a problem. Generally, it is men who believe this - "I'll just let her talk it out and eventually she'll leave me alone." Nothing could be further from the truth! I remember a client reporting that she was very upset with her husband, and was trying to talk about it with him. Though she could tell he was paying attention because he was looking at her, he made no response. Frustrated, she made her point again, a bit more strongly this time. Once again, when he said nothing, she reiterated the point with greater intensity. After the third "round" of this, she finally said, "Don't think that just because you're not saying anything, you're not contributing to this argument!" She had been made to feel completely unimportant.

Resentment can, of course, manifest in fighting. How often do you find that you and your spouse are entangled in arguments that really make no sense? These conflicts seem to take on a life of their own, bitterness prevails on each side, energy is depleted, and no one quite wins. The only thing that seems certain is that neither of you is sure what you were arguing about.

All of these have a profound impact. Naturally, they hurt the recipient. Internal resentment also builds in the person acting negatively, so (s)he also suffers. Oddly, the person may be oblivious that this is occurring. The result is a perpetuation of the feeling and probably to a greater extent than what existed previously. The heightened emotionality then acts as a filtering system for future interaction, leading to a spiraling effect of still greater resentment.

No matter in what form an attack comes, it always displays disrespect for the other person. Unfortunately, part of our comfort level includes taking one another for granted and forgetting that our partner is a person, too, with feelings and sensitivities.

No doubt, in our relationships, each of us has suffered some hurt at some point. It is often hard to let go of these feelings. But if you want to have a smoother relationship, it is helpful to think in terms of "winning the war and not the battle." It is very important to remember the benefit of not attacking each other and keeping a perspective of a harmonious relationship as compared to always being right. The only thing that happens when someone is attacked is that (s)he needs to protect (her)himself - it is a natural instinct. (Only a masochist would ask for more.) When we feel attacked, our emotions flare up - we might feel hurt or angry. Those are strong feelings that demand our attention and, therefore, get in the way of any rational, logical thinking. Since logic is not operational at this point, clear thinking is not available. So, too, does listening get compromised since listening is a rational, cognitive skill. Can you remember back to when you were in school and your teacher said something that did not make sense? You raised your hand for clarification but she chose to talk a bit more before she responded to you. Did you hear the rest of what she said? No, because there was an emotional level of frustration that clouded your ability to comprehend the words she continued to speak. This process is exactly what happens. So, if you want your partner to be receptive to what you have to say, do not attack. In summary, when an attack takes place, the other person protects him or herself and virtually stops attending to you, essentially bringing to a halt any form of productive communication.

There is research now that is addressing the role that the brain plays in one's emotionality. At birth, a small almond-shaped part of the brain, the amygdala, is present. Its role is to help the organism survive by sensing danger. When there is a potential threat to the organism, the amygdala goes into a "fight/flight" syndrome, either attacking the threatening object or fleeing from it. Very protective. The cortex, or thinking, rational part of the brain does not really start to develop until a child is two, and continues to learn rational components for many years to come. If a situation somehow "reminds" the amygdala of something threatening, it will, in an attempt to protect the person, go into immediate reaction before the cortex has the chance to rationally figure out if this stimulus is, in fact, the same or different. That is, is the stimulus to which one is reacting, in reality, harmful? This physiological explanation offers us a fuller understanding as to why people react as they do (often irrationally). It is also useful from the perspective of the interactions that take place in a relationship. If an intense reaction is triggered, it makes a lot more sense to call a "time-out." This will stop the argument from escalating. It is better to leave things alone for a while and come back to the discussion later.

Also beneficial is making a firm pact that there will be no name-calling, no belittling, or dredging up all sorts of other outside issues. The idea of timing your discussions will be an essential skill to increase "fair fighting." It is essential in any relationship to develop the skill of "active listening ." In essence this means listening at a deeper level, so that you are paying attention to the words as well as the *feelings* beneath the words. Active listening will be much more useful at a point where both parties can respect one another as well as the other's opinions and feelings.

Ongoing built-up resentment can be very damaging to the relationship. It is hard to break through since it is really an accumulation of several other pent-up emotions. Typically, since we feel less vulnerable when we're resentful, it may be easier to still remain functional. Therefore, resentment affords us a real sense of protection. Resentment also seems to offer a sense of entitlement. You can easily point to what the other person did or did not do that creates this feeling in you. Because of these behaviors on the part of your spouse, it seems fair that you can express your resentment either actively or passively. "How many times do I have to ask him to bring up the laundry because my back is killing me? Well, I'll just show him and forget to pick up his prescription at the drugstore!" "You keep nagging me to change the fixture. I'll get to it. Don't you realize how tiring it is to work all day?" Or, if you are being honest, how often do you pretend not to hear your partner's request because "you've had it!" The examples of resentment statements are countless.

For some couples, resentment and anger leads to dramatic consequences; for others, there is a creation of a wall of silence. In either situation, there is a rapid erosion to the relationship.

Years ago, a client entered her session telling me how proud I would be of her because she had many emotional reactions to her husband during the week to which she did not respond. Rather, she swallowed them. But swallowed, or unexpressed emotions, do not disappear. At some point, in some way, they do get expressed - usually non-productively. One of the typical consequences of holding emotions in is that when finally approaching your partner, you approach with what is considered a "harsh start-up." This basically means that you raise the issue in an attacking manner.

So what do you do with all the feelings or concerns you have? Do they go unaddressed? Absolutely not!

There are some key guidelines that will have a positive impact on effective communication:

1) Do not disrespect your partner's views or emotions by referring to them as "meaningless" or "idiotic" or any other criticism.

2) Talk at a time when the intensity has cooled down.

3) Often the problem can be neutralized by referring to it in a generic vs. specific manner (e.g. "it").

4) It's very important to embrace the concept that the other person is not "bad," just different from you. If you can work from the standpoint that you and your mate are different from one another, it precludes the idea that one of you is right and one of you is wrong. It will allow you to not feel so hurt or angry when (s)he does not see things or do things the way you would. A more accepting attitude will allow you to approach your mate in a kinder, less attacking way. As this attitude and consequential behavior gets going, you will start to see a kinder attitude coming back to you. This, then, allows for appropriate, more respectful, and compassionate feelings for each other. Certainly, this approach will bring back more of the vibrancy to the relationship.

Resentment/Anger Exercises:

12a. When you are feeling angry, it will be very helpful to think about what is causing this feeling. Ask yourself the following questions:

- If you really examine your feelings, are there other emotions that are underneath the anger?

- What are the chances your mate meant to *intentionally* create that feeling in you? In other words, was this a conscious effort on his or her part?

- What meaning did the upsetting behavior have to you? What triggers does it have for you?

- What other explanations are possible for why your partner did the behavior that is angering you?

12b. If you have difficulty answering the questions in "a," think back to a time where the situation was reversed; that is, when your partner was angry because of something you did or did not do. Recall what the circumstances were from your perspective. We always, naturally, understand more of the particulars when it is about us. We have more information about our own lives, especially our intentions. Think back to a time when you were well meaning but your partner was still upset; it is easier to see how there can be a gap between what was meant to be communicated and how something was taken.

It often helps to view a similar situation when "the shoe was on the other foot." By having this insight, it will help you consider that there is another explanation for your partner's behavior, other than the conclusion you have come to.

12c. Now it's time to become more aware of *your* communication to your partner. You cannot change something if you are not aware of it. Therefore, it is essential that you become aware of the things you say to your partner that can be perceived as attacks.

Sometimes, this will be easy to do because you see your partner's reaction. So, if you say something and your mate's face or body expression changes, your mate gets quiet, or your mate verbally attacks you, it generally means your mate has felt attacked. If any of these things happens try the following:

** Stop what you are doing and saying (which may have caused the negative reaction you observed in your mate).

** Check with your mate by describing what you've observed (e.g. "I notice that your arms are folded across your chest. Have I said something that had a negative effect on you?").

** If your mate denies that anything is wrong, continue what you are saying, still observing his or her reaction. If you again see a nonverbal negative reaction, try to restate your point a different way by saying, "Let me try to say this differently this time."

12d.   Perhaps, you aren't even aware that you come across in an attacking way. Every time we communicate with someone, we do it with our words, tone of voice, and body language. Communication with your mate will be improved as you become more aware of how each of these variables impacts the listener. Using a piece of paper, make a list of 3 people with whom you regularly communicate (one of these should be your mate). Do the following:

** Along the left margin of the paper write each person's name in a column. Along the top of the paper make 4 columns labeled: **words, tone of voice, body language,** and **effect on me.**

** Over the course of one week (or longer if needed), go back to your paper and note an interaction you had with each of the three people you identified. For each interaction write down as much as you can remember about **a sentence or question** they said, how they sounded, and how they looked. **You don't need the whole conversation,** but just select one or two things you remember that they said to you.

** Now complete the fourth column and try to remember the <u>effect</u> each of these people had on <u>you</u>.

** Now it's your turn. Practice (by yourself vs. actually speaking to these people) saying one or two sentences back to each of these people while standing in front of the mirror. Go back to your paper and fill in the words you used, your tone of voice, your body language and what effect you think you would have on *them*. As you practice your response, decide *how* you want your message to come across (e.g. understanding, concerned, loving, etc.). Since this is a practice exercise, you may want to tape record yourself as you practice and then play it back to assess if the way you sound is the way you intended to sound. This will build your confidence for when you actually do deliver your message the next time.

12f.   If you have had an interaction with your mate that was unpleasant, a couple of hours later, reflect back on it. Replay the incident in your head. You need to wait at least a couple of hours so that you can reflect objectively, without your emotions getting in the way.

The more often you try this exercise, the better you will be at identifying your attacking behavior which will be a major step toward doing something different.

12g. Whether you are the one who got angry or your partner is the angry one, it's important to talk to each other about the incident. Talking always gets better results when the emotion has subsided. (So, if you're the one who's angry, remember to do "a" and "b," first; if your partner is angry, exercises "c" and "d" should be done before discussion.)

If you are still too angry, it will be difficult to have a talk that will truly be productive.

You can always bring something up later; a *calm* discussion that is delayed will be a much more worthwhile one. Raise the issue by stating objective facts rather than either of you attacking each other about what was done or not done. Certainly express your feelings making sure to say they are *your* feelings. (In the section of the book about communication skills, there are a great deal more details on how to approach your partner so that communication is effective.)

12h. If, in the past, you have been the type to not respond to issues your mate brings up, offer a response. A response which indicates that you do not quite know *how* to respond, is better than *no* response at all.

THIRTEEN

RESISTANCE

Scenario 13

Bob is at work and a colleague of his, Joe, just offered him two tickets to a baseball game this weekend that Joe can't attend. Bob accepts the tickets and calls Sue at work.

SUE: Hello, this is Sue. How may I help you?

BOB: Hi, babe, guess who?

SUE: Well, this is a nice surprise in the middle of the day, honey. Everything okay?

BOB: Can't a man call his wife just because?

SUE: Of course he can. Now, tell me what's goin' on. You sound excited.

BOB: I have good news...Joe has to handle a big account and go out of town this weekend. As a result, we have just inherited two tickets to the baseball game. They're great seats, I might add!

SUE: Oh...that sounds great except -

BOB: Except what?

SUE: I told the kids we'd all go to the opening of the new amusement park this weekend.

BOB: Okay, no problem. We can just go to the park Sunday or any other weekend they want.

SUE: It's not that easy. The kids both have other plans for Sunday and the opening day is kind of a special event with a parade that they don't want to miss.

BOB: Sue, you know what a huge baseball fan I am, and these tickets are incredible. The kids will understand or maybe they could go with your parents.

SUE: Bob, I know you're not happy about it but a promise is a promise. Maybe you want to ask one of the guys at work if they - (Bob interrupts her).

BOB: Nah, there's no one I'd really want to go with. Besides, I thought this would be a fun, spontaneous thing for us to do. You always put the kids' needs before me, Sue, and I'm getting tired of it.

SUE: Now wait a minute, that's not really true. I do my best to balance your needs and the kids' needs. Plus, we have to be good role models and breaking a promise isn't such a great thing to model.

BOB: So, what does that mean, you're "Miss Perfect Parent" and I'm not? All I'm asking is for you to be more spontaneous once in a while. Is that a crime?

SUE: You have a short memory. I've changed plans in the past so we could do something that was important to you. Now because I'm sticking to my plans this time, you won't let go of the issue.

BOB: If the tables were turned, Sue, you'd feel the same way. Think about it.

SUE: I am thinking about it and what I think is that you're being childish. Maybe you need to grow up, Bob!

A very important outlook is to accept that no one or no relationship is perfect. Though most of us can acknowledge that point as a positive attitude, when an imperfection is obvious, we often feel let down or hurt. Generally, it is not a fault of the person, but rather a fault in the way we are thinking and perceiving. If there are times you react because of your expectation of perfection, it would be much more beneficial to question yourself and discover why the situation feels so bad to you. It may very well be that you were hoping your mate would fulfill something that feels empty to you. Perhaps, the disappointment is really directed at your mate. She may, in the past, have always acted a certain way and the change is upsetting. In this case, the expectation has been set up because your partner has consistently acted a certain way, thus leading you to expect that she will continue to act similarly. From time to time, for a number of reasons, someone may not live up to his or her usual performance. In either case, it is important to look at the bigger picture. By focusing on a specific incident, we tend to lose site of the overall circumstances.

The following scenario presents a good illustration. Years ago, a client was planning her daughter's wedding. Among the guests was a close friend whom she always invited to special occasions. He had recently remarried. Though he initially replied that he would attend, he called to say that he would not be able to come. She was aghast and highly insulted. How could he! After all, he had always been a part of her special times and this would be the first function he missed! She was upset for days. When we discussed it, I pointed out that this was the only occasion he had missed - why did she focus on that rather than the fact that he had always been there for everything else. When she looked at it that way, the hurt vanished.

A related concept is the acceptance of "good enough." This does not necessarily mean that you always have to settle for mediocre. But if you come to terms with the idea that very few things are perfect, it will allow you to enjoy and appreciate what is. Relationships (as well as life) mean compromise and sacrifice. If you view these aspects as settling or giving in, you will lose out on whatever positive exists. If you can accept that nothing is perfect, you are much more likely to reap the benefits that come your way.

Another very important aspect to making your relationship work is that of forgiveness. I am not suggesting that you automatically forgive your partner if there has been a hurt. It's important to talk about the feelings, to process what happened so that you can each understand the other better. If your partner is truly sorry, then it is in your *own* best interest and that of the relationship to forgive. That does not mean that you forget what took place. But to hold on to anger takes a lot of energy; energy that is then not available for yourself or the relationship.

All relationships have problems and conflicts. Since you are two different people with different sets of backgrounds, needs, and emotions, there are bound to be periodic problems.   A couple who seemingly never has any problems is either not being truly honest with one another, or feels too uncomfortable with conflict. It has been found that the main predictor as to whether a marriage lasts is the couple's ability to tolerate having conflict with one another. When a couple escapes conflict and pretends that everything is harmonious, the relationship is weakened (Roberts, 2000). There are times when you will argue and, in fact, that is healthy. But when the arguing gets nasty and hurtful, damage can be done.

Though many of you have heard the expression, "fair fighting," most people do not really understand what that means. A few simple rules will allow for venting and disagreeing yet still maintaining respect and dignity. Using words or phrases that attack the other person is definitely taboo. The point can certainly be made without resorting to name-calling.

Also, it is important that you stick to the topic that was raised and not dredge up past concerns that you "pull out of the hat." So, if the argument is about visiting someone's family again, discuss that and the feelings and thoughts about that topic only. This is not the time to bring up how insulted you felt about the gift a family member brought the last time they came over. In fact, the gift issue may be one that is unresolved for you and needs attention - but not at this time. To bring up all sorts of unrelated topics creates chaos and does not allow for clarification of the initial point.

There are times that an argument will get heated and emotions are running high. It is hard to communicate in any meaningful way when this happens. It might be a good idea for a "time-out." But it is also a good idea to state that you are taking a time-out rather than just walking out. To do so will most likely be perceived as abandonment or withdrawal.

Sometimes, a situation may not be able to be resolved immediately. As stated above, there may be too much emotion involved. It is very hard to be really listening and understanding your partner when you are so upset. Or, even if there was not an argument, you may realize at some later time that something you said was not communicated in the best way possible. I believe strongly in the concept of "repair work." Just because some time has elapsed, whether it is an hour, a day, or even a week, going back to the situation and discussing your realization can be very helpful to the relationship. So, even if a problem is not handled well at the time it is happening, by going back to it, there is a larger gain. By revisiting a problem it sends the message to your partner that you care which, in and of itself, will help build a sense of connection.   Talking, understanding, growing, and healing are taking place. By being willing to think about it and come back to the problem sends a message that says, "I think about us, I care."

Resistance Exercises:

13a. Often a good time to develop a game plan or strategy is when you and your mate are communicating well. Plan to set aside a time to sit down together and "brainstorm" ground rules that are important to each of you when you have an argument. Remember that with brainstorming all ideas are acceptable and censoring is avoided. One of you should take the role of writing these ideas down on a pad of paper.

13b. Once the brainstorming is complete (you cannot think of any other ideas) then each of you should look over the list of ideas and agree to a set of "ground rules" that you will each try to follow when you have an argument. Examples of ground rules could include: I will not use name-calling, I will not make insulting comments, I will not walk out of the room, I will announce I need a time-out or break to let my mate know what I am doing, I will not drag up old concerns, etc.

13c. The agreed upon ground rules should be printed legibly and posted in a location where they can easily be viewed (you may also want to each have your own copy).

13d. Make a commitment to one another that when arguments occur, each of you will take responsibility to review the ground rules as close to the time of the argument as possible. You can even try to tell one another to do so at the time of the argument if you can.

13e. Assuming you do not review the ground rules as the argument occurs, go back to review them after the argument and rate yourself to see where you went off task.

Consider this like being a movie critic who gives a review of a movie. Write down what you did that was positive and what you did that needs improvement. Share this information with your mate and gently encourage him or her to use the same process.

13f. Offer an apology to your mate for any ground rule that you did not follow.

FOURTEEN

BACKSLIDING

Scenario 14

Bob has recently learned that in light of not meeting budget expectations, his company may be anticipating downsizing, which he has shared with Sue.

SUE: Ya' know, Bob, I was speaking to some of the women at work today and they were telling me about some great benefits to having vacation timeshares.

BOB: Those wouldn't work for us.

SUE: Well, I'm not so sure. I thought it would be fun to attend a seminar this month to learn more about them and get some facts. Sound good?

BOB: Count me out! I'm not wasting my time at one of those stupid

seminars.

SUE: I just thought it was a good way to learn about a vacation option

and it doesn't obligate us in any way. C'mon....please.

BOB: No means no, Sue. Looking at vacation options is the last thing I

want to be doing right now.

SUE: You used to get so excited about these kinds of things. Lately, you

pooh-pooh just about every idea I come up with.

BOB: I'd like to see you take on the problems I have at work and not get

a little depressed.

SUE: If it were a *little* it wouldn't be so bad. But it keeps getting worse

and worse.

BOB: What are you saying?

SUE: You had problems with your depression in the first year of our

marriage. I thought we had worked them out, but it looks like

they're back.

BOB: So what do you want from me?

SUE: How about looking on the bright side of things once in awhile, like you

used to after your therapy - instead of always taking the dark view?

When people have worked hard to accomplish a goal, and that goal is pretty much satisfied, it is easy to want to take a rest and fall back on the accomplishments. This is very natural and well-deserved. You have worked hard and have accomplished something that is so important. And, in fact, credit is due. However, to think in terms of being done would be the quickest way to set yourself up for future problems. It is important to remember that your relationship is one which must take priority and one which will require constant attention and nurturing. The premise of this book is that in order for a relationship to stay vibrant, it must be prioritized. By reading this far, you have learned tools to restore the vibrancy to your relationship. Committing to some final skills will help prevent you from backsliding. In so doing this will enable your relationship to thrive.

Though you have realized how essential it is to be mindful of your relationship, that awareness will not totally shield you. It is unrealistic to think that there will be no outside stresses impacting your relationship. As you have seen in the past, stress is a natural part of life and of any relationship; therefore, knowing how to work with it will be a valuable tool. By definition, stress is a feeling that results when there are things to cope with that we perceive as overwhelming or beyond our capability of dealing with. Stress, though often negative, also includes positive events; pleasant as they might be, they too require coping. So, as an example, as your first child begins kindergarten, feeling stressed on an emotional and practical level would be quite normal. There may be concerns about buying the right clothes or the correct school supplies. If there is a younger sibling, how will you take this child to school while the baby is still asleep? Or, as another example, if either you or your mate is taking classes, exam time is likely be to a stressful period for each of you, though in different ways. So, it is vital that you realize that stress is a part of life. What you want to try and maintain is a balance in your life. If one of you is anticipating a hectic period, perhaps the other one can pick up more of the responsibilities. If you know that things will be difficult for a certain period of time, plan a getaway at the end of that period, so that you have something to look forward to as well as what will be a welcome rest. It would be quite common for the person who is stressed to be irritable or short on patience. This can even happen without the person being aware of it. Rather than react, make inquiries that are understanding and caring. Though difficult, it is very helpful if the unstressed person does not personalize the other's stressed-out behavior. That will only add to and perpetuate the stress. It may be helpful to give each person a short gripe period each evening. It helps to break the stress and clear the tension. It is probable that, at times, other things will come first. Or, there may be times when, because one or both of you are stressed, that you cannot give your all to the relationship. These deviations have to be expected by realizing that they are all part of the package.

To expect a perfect relationship at all times is a dream. Slips will happen. I always tell my clients who are leaving therapy that they are not "cured" and that they must expect that problems will arise. Problems are part of life. They help us grow because they present challenges. The tools presented in this book provide skills that will better equip you in managing your relationship. These tools are for *when* problems happens, not *if* they happen. You have worked hard and have learned a lot that can help you. Should some backsliding (reverting back to old behaviors) occur, recognize it as a slip; do not feel you have lost what you learned. All is not lost - you need only to implement the tools you've learned in this book again.

Backsliding Exercises:

14a. At least once a day, say, "Thank you" to your partner. It does not have to be for anything big. As a matter of fact, being appreciated for small things is very meaningful. Here are a couple of ideas in case you are stuck: "Thank you for picking up my clothes at the cleaner," "Thanks for putting gas in my car," "Thanks for reminding me about that appointment."

14b. Several times during the week, make sure to praise or compliment your partner. Remember, if you are hoping to have your partner respond differently, change will take place in small, gradual steps. Therefore, you want to praise anything that is more in line with what you would like (if reinforcement is held out until perfection is achieved, the improvements will never occur). If your mate is always a half hour late, but this time is only 15 minutes late, thank them for their effort.

14c. Take a few moments to verbalize the things you like about your partner to him or her. Being open and sharing positive feelings will put a good spin on how you relate to each other - it sets the stage for looking for the good and not letting the negative mean so much.

14d. Plan to spend time together. A bonus would be to do so spontaneously. Can you imagine the message that is sent if you approach your mate and say, "Let's go for a drive, I can get to that project later." And while you are together, do not forget to think back on where your relationship was three months ago as compared to where it is now. Sometimes when progress is small and steady, it is hard to see the change.

This type of reflection helps you see the progress you've made. By being aware of how much more vibrant your relationship has become, it is reinforcing in its own right and a real booster to keep it up.

SUMMARY

Remember how you dreaded practicing scales on the piano, memorizing multiplication tables or even riding your new two-wheeler? What started out to be initially difficult, soon be came second nature and ultimately your efforts paid off. And just like your experience with your two-wheeler, if you don't keep riding, your skills become rusty. But they do return to you once you make them a priority. So it can be with your marriage.

There are some things you can do to ensure you measure your progress and stay on course. Reminisce about how the relationship *used* to be and compare it to how it is *now*. This helps remind you how far you have come and what you've accomplished. Feel free to point out to each other, after handling a situation well, about how you used to handle the same situation in the past. Be generous with your compliments or reinforcements to your partner as well as to yourself. Doing so helps to strengthen your new behavior and makes it the rule rather than the exception.

And remember to have fun! Tools and effort are both important and essential in a working relationship. But working *too* much can also make a relationship become tired and dull. Fun is a very important ingredient to keeping a relationship going; keeping it spontaneous, fresh - preventing it from becoming stale.

So, when you think back on where your relationship was before you read this book, it may have initially seemed overwhelming, if not impossible to make a change. But with consistent attention you see that the challenge is one that you can master. With continued attention what you will find is that working on your relationship becomes easier. With time you will work your way back to a relationship that offers the two of you satisfaction, joy, and fun.

PART THREE

ONE

COMMUNICATION CONCEPTS

Communication! It's a relationship tool that everybody recognizes as valuable. When things start to go wrong, it's something that we can identify as missing. And, unfortunately, it is a skill that very few of us really know how to implement when it is most needed.

Research has shown that with 87% accuracy, it can be predicted which newlywed couples will divorce. This prediction is based on how they talk to each other rather than what they actually say. Communication may very well be the most important skill in a relationship. The ability to communicate ideas or concepts is what separates us from the lower species of animals. We need this skill to allow us to relate to each other, starting with the simple tasks of informing one another about the day-to-day concerns in a relationship - what time we will meet for dinner, who will do what chore, the business and social commitments we have. It is the vehicle that allows us to learn about our partner, and the one through which we reveal ourselves. It's the way we let each other know what our needs are, or when something doesn't feel right. And yet, because most of us do not communicate well, it is the reason our relationships so often suffer.

Before we go on to offer tools that will help to make your communication skills better, it is helpful to understand why there is so much difficulty in this area. As with other issues, when we do not understand the rationale for differences, we often assign it to mean that the other person does not care. It seems that if they did care, they would be much more "in sync" with us. Their understanding and appreciation of us would be manifested by clear communication. However, there are lots of explanations as to why communication could be "off" having nothing to do with another person caring for us.

Again, keep in mind that people have been raised differently. Some come from homes that encouraged expressing thoughts and feelings; in other homes, these values were not stressed. For example, some children learn quickly that the expression of emotion is not well received in their family. Additionally, if, as a child, the parent responded negatively or harshly when the child was emotional, it will not feel "safe" to reveal feelings later in life. Others may have been told that unless you have something nice to say, it shouldn't be said at all. The early lessons in life are usually carried over into adulthood. Therefore, whatever styles of communicating were taught in the home will be brought into adult relationships. When people are hesitant to express themselves, the task is a little more difficult, though not impossible by any means. It will require a little more risk taking. This can be a much easier task if encouraged by the partner. But encouragement means just that - not demanding or insisting. Secondly, regardless of whether someone has come from an open or closed background, it is unlikely that someone will be open in their communication if they are met with a negative or judgmental response.

The difference in communication styles between men and women is well known. There is some biological research indicating that females have far greater vocalizations than males. Others suggest that it is because as infants, women were spoken to more frequently. Therefore, they learn that verbalizing and attending to verbalizations are important. Additionally, they tend to be process-oriented: paying attention to the internal aspects of the family and how everyone is feeling. Men, in contrast, are more action-oriented. They have not learned to pay attention to words or the subtleties of expression (facial cues, gestures, or voice intonation). Rather, men have been reinforced for what they do; success is based on the proverbial "bottom line." And though things are changing, most men have been told as boys to not express emotion. This action-oriented approach extends to the manner in which men offer help. Rather than giving some form of emotional support, they will come up with a number of solutions to the presented problem. Since they are results-oriented, they will focus more attention on the external needs of the family, like paying the bills. Women also tend to speak in ways that are more specific to what they intend. For instance, when a woman says, "I'll call you later," you can expect that you will, indeed, hear from her later. A man, however, making the same statement could mean later that day, tomorrow, next week, or even as an alternate way of saying "good-bye." Given these different experiences and influences, is it any wonder that there would be such disparity as people of the opposite sex communicate?

In fact, when interacting, the differences in the communication styles between men and women become exceedingly apparent. Not only are the differences there initially but they actually further perpetuate the gap. Men are generally not predisposed to initiating dialogue or even responding in elaborate ways. Women, in response to this, tend to ask more of their mate. The "request" can be as mild as more attempts to engage their partner or more to asking questions of him, or to making attacks on his *perceived* minimal interest. Though not every woman interprets a man's silence as a lack of interest, great majorities do, and some will take it to mean that the man doesn't care. Regardless of the meaning a woman attaches to a man's lesser communication, there is some level of dissatisfaction that is conveyed. This communication can occur non-verbally through body language, facial expressions, or gestures. And when people are close to one another, they are emotionally attuned to "reading" one another's emotional signals. So, whether acknowledged or not, the dissatisfaction is uncomfortable. Generally, when someone is uncomfortable they resort to doing more of whatever does feel comfortable. For most men, comfort is likely to be achieved by withdrawing. Do you start to see the pattern that develops? As a man withdraws, a woman will reach out even more, only to have the man withdraw even further. And so on, and so on, and so on. Eventually, a "dance" such as this can only lead to stepping on one another's toes and probably a decision to sit it out all together. A man's stonewalling (not responding to his mate) has been found in research to be one of the five negative behaviors that is toxic to a marriage. Of course, stonewalling is not gender-specific; women can also do it. Regardless of which one of the two withdraws, the eventual outcome is a shutdown of the communication process. Withdrawing can be as corrosive to the relationship as blatant hostility. At the very least, it is essential that a man be willing to listen to what his mate is saying. Of equal importance is a woman presenting what she has to say in a way that is non-attacking or what is known as a harsh start-up. The latter is one of the indicators of a couple who may likely divorce. Rather, it is far more beneficial to raise subjects of concern in a gentle way and even with making some positive comments (something that will be discussed in detail later).

To make matters even more complicated, people also differ in their use of language. Communication is made up of two parts - sending and receiving. It turns out that each of us has a favored modality in which we express ourselves and receive input. Read the following sentences to see if you detect the differences:

a. I really sense that you have a problem in this area. I feel I can be helpful to you.

b. I really see that this is a problem for you. Let's look at some solutions I can offer.

c. I really hear that this is a problem for you. It sounds like something I can help you with.

Though the three examples virtually express the same points, they differ in the choice of modality. In order of presentation, the modalities are kinesthetic (feel), visual (see), and auditory (hear). If you did not pick these differences up, go back and read the sentences again. Many times, two people will have a problem communicating because they are not employing the same modality. It is like trying to use push-button calling with a rotary phone. If you are not aware that this problem could be happening, the conversation may end up being very frustrating.

Continuing along the line of sending and receiving, even if as the sender, you believe you are being articulate, it is quite possible that the way you have phrased something is just not getting across. To repeat it in the same way will not get a different result. If you realize that you are not being understood, it would make good communication sense to change your message. Sometimes when something is presented differently, it will be heard differently as well.

Another "misfire" occurs because people do not have the ability to hear hints. For relationships, this inability could create a lot of difficulty. Especially for women who value a man being "tuned into her," dropping a hint with the expectation that he will pick it up can lead to serious damage.

New research reveals further complications for this issue. It seems that when women listen, both hemispheres of the brain are activated. Conversely, when a man listens, only one hemisphere is employed. Since each hemisphere tends to specialize either in emotion or logic, a man is either processing information emotionally *or* cognitively - but not both at the same time as a woman does! So while it's understandable that a woman feels she's not being listened to, it's important to acknowledge that this is a physiological difference rather than an intentional behavior on the man's part. However, the situation is not a hopeless one. Listening skills can be learned and the exercises provided in this book help to compensate for this difference.

Communication skills are usually lacking because they were never really learned. Similar to the other skills, poor communication becomes a habit. In order to change it, you must become aware of better ways of communicating and work at becoming more comfortable in using these newly acquired skills.

Clearly, it is an erroneous assumption that just because we speak the same language, we will understand one another. To do so is not an easy task. And it is unlikely that perfection in communication will ever happen. But learning to communicate better is quite possible, and we offer the following skills to help. As you go through the skills, remember that when you learn anything new it takes time and the acceptance of the premise that both you and your partner will make mistakes. Either we never learned certain skills or we learned them incorrectly. In either case, the willingness to revise and improve now is what is important. It is a clear statement about the importance of your relationship.

QUICK REFERENCE TO COMMUNICATION CONCEPTS

- People are raised in different families and therefore will have different lifestyle expectations.

- Men and women are brought up to attend to the world from different perspectives: men are action-oriented whereas women are more concerned with process.

- Women's language is specific to their intention while men speak in greater generalities.

- Women initiate and are more active in conversation, whereas men tend to be less communicative.

- Communication is both expressive and receptive and people tend to favor a particular modality in their communication (kinesthetic, visual, or auditory).

- When a message isn't being understood, consider changing your presentation.

- People vary in their ability to be aware of hints - women are usually better at this.

- Communication skills have been and can be relearned to be more effective.

TWO

COMMUNICATION TOOLS

Now that you have a greater understanding of why communication can run so amuck, let's move on to the skills that will put you back on track. As has been said before, good communication takes two people cooperating with each other. The person receiving the information is very instrumental as to whether the information is shared. Effective communication involves both the expression of (sending) and listening to (receiving) the message. A key to listening is realizing that it is *more* than simply hearing the words someone is saying. The goal is to *actively* listen versus hear, which is more of a passive act. When *actively* listening, you paraphrase, acknowledge or feed back to the speaker that you've understood what they've said. So, if you want your partner to open up, make sure you provide an attitude that is open to hearing, to learning, to understanding - not one that is merely looking for agreement or a similar point of view. When your partner is communicating to you, whether it concerns your relationship or something else, embrace the idea of respecting one another's thoughts, feelings, and opinions. All too often, when our partner expresses an idea that is different than the one we have, we are closed down to it. Not only are we not receptive, but in many cases, we are judgmental. Try to reframe, to think differently about, your partner's seemingly "idiotic" or "silly" opinion as a different point of view; a point of view that deserves respect. If you think about the kind of response *you* would like from your partner, it may be easier to offer the same back. Imagine a time when you told someone something and they were less than positive in receiving it. How did that feel? Were you likely to want to share more about this topic - or any other for that matter? When we are hurt or upset with our partner, we are likely to convey these feelings but generally do so in less than productive ways. This might include shutting down and not talking at all. Certainly, these behaviors are contrary to keeping communication open.

Perhaps one of the biggest difficulties in relationships is that one or both partners are hesitant to state or ask for that they want from the partner. Though not always, more stereotypically, women have a harder time with this practice. It is as if the ability to anticipate or know the other's needs without being told is indicative of caring. And though, in fact, it may signify caring and careful attention, *not* knowing does not mean that the care is not there. Too often, the reluctance to ask has more to do with a sense of vulnerability. After all, if something is not directly requested, it cannot be directly rejected. How many times have you noticed that your mate was upset and when you asked, "What's wrong?" the answer was "If you don't know I'm not going to tell you!" However, most of us are not mind readers and to assess the satisfaction in your relationship based on this hope is really doing yourself an injustice. It is important to let go of this fantasy and make a clear statement about your needs. If you make a direct request, there is a greater likelihood that it will be met since the request can be understood. Think of how good it will feel to ask for something and have the need heard and responded to.

However, making the statement does not necessarily mean that all your needs will be met. To assume so is equally erroneous. It is quite demanding and selfish to expect your needs to be totally met because your needs may not be consistent with those of your partner. If you do ask directly for what you need and your partner is not able to respond as you would like, the next step toward good communication would be to ask, "Why?" rather than make your own assumptions. Most likely, unspoken assumptions will lead toward the feeling that your partner doesn't care about you. Rather, if you ask about your partner's unwillingness to oblige, you are likely to hear something that is unrelated to you not being cared about.

Since asking is a skill that many of us are uncomfortable with, when one attempts to do so, the verbalization that is expressed is often a demand rather than a request. Here are some examples:

A. "Make sure you call me before you leave." (Demanding)

B. "Do you mind calling me before you leave? I'd really appreciate it." (Requesting)

Demands come across as controlling and few people like to feel that they are being controlled. Therefore, people are not as likely to respond favorably to a demand; if they do so, there is likely to be some residual resentment. Try to be aware of how you are coming across. Your partner may give you cues that she is not comfortable with your request; as indicated by a facial expression or a resistance to the request. If you become aware that your request may not have gone over well, use it as an opportunity to talk to each other, to learn about one another's communication styles, needs, and feelings. What may start out as unpleasant may lead you to some very productive communication.

A variation of asking has to do with hidden expectations. We come to expect things in our world to be consistent with the way we were raised. But since there is a very good chance that you and your partner were not raised in exactly the same way, there will be differences in what each of you expects. If not expressed, a real problem can ensue. As an example, let's say that your mate was raised in a family where birthday celebrations were no big deal. The birthday was always acknowledged either on the actual day or the weekend, depending on when it was easier. Your mate had her eye on something she wanted, told her family, and that became the gift. In your family, birthdays were a big celebration. They were always celebrated on the actual day and gifts were a fun surprise; family members made purchases by having paid close attention to hints. With the knowledge that birthdays were no big deal for your partner, to maintain the expectation that she will make a big deal without you making your expectations known is setting yourself up for a big disappointment. It is important to remember that your partner is behaving in a way that is consistent with his or her experiences and it is not an indication of not caring. Being more open about your expectations will allow for greater intimacy. The more open the relationship is, the more alive it will feel.

An extremely important skill is that of validation. In short, this concept means that you let the other person know that you understand *his or her* point of view. You do not have to agree with it, you merely have to be able to comprehend where (s)he is "coming from." Then you are able to offer empathy rather than sympathy. Imagine you and your partner are outside when a car accident takes place. The police come to take your eyewitness testimony. The chances are very good that each of you will give slightly different reports. That is not because either one of you is lying, but simply because you are two different people with two different perspectives. Sounds pretty logical, doesn't it? Yet, when it comes to our relating to each other's point of view, we forget this. Our different histories act as filters resulting in our seeing and responding to the world differently.

Validation is a very significant skill in that it promotes the ability for communication to continue. If a person is not validated, not understood, it is likely that (s)he will feel frustrated. Various reactions can result from feeling this way. Some people will shut down and feel resentful; others may continue talking and trying to make the same point clear by presenting it over and over again. In either case, it is likely that each partner will come away from the experience unsatisfied in some way. A common mistake that is made, stereotypically by men, works against the feeling of validation. The male gender is raised to be problem-solvers; therefore, a man will often offer a solution to a problem when his female partner comes to him to discuss something. The woman, having been raised to be a caretaker, will not feel satisfied or appreciative of the offering. Consequently, the man feels clueless and perhaps upset that his help was rejected. Neither is happy. A more validating response on the part of the man would be to offer a display of sincere concern, with no solution provided. Here's an example:

SUE: "I really feel I'm not getting paid enough for the job I do."

BOB's response:

A. "Why don't you tell your boss it's time for a raise?" (Problem-solving response)

B. "You really do work hard." (Validating response)

Even just one's physical presence with focused listening is a gift of self that is both validating and healing.

Communication does not mean merely expressing an idea or giving a piece of information, whether that information is factual or personal. *It really is a vehicle for coming to understand the other person and having the other person understand you.* To reach this goal, it may take a bit of unraveling. This unraveling concept is called processing. Fundamentally, processing consists of truly listening, explaining, and becoming aware of the points at which things got mixed up. We often assume that because we speak the same language, we know what the other person has meant or that they know what we mean. Too often, there are hurt feelings and consequential actions based on those feelings which are the result of a misunderstood communication. I am reminded of a female client who was really upset because she and her boyfriend were to spend the day together. At 5 o'clock, he dropped her off to spend the rest of the evening with his buddies. Was he uncaring? Was she demanding? Neither was the case - they just never took the time to be clear about exactly what each of them meant by the phrase "spend the day." She goes on to be hurt but does not clarify that she is. But, the next time they get together, she has an attitude. Since he has no idea why she is upset with him and cannot think of anything he has done, he assumes it is something personal that is upsetting her and, therefore, does not ask.

(At this point, some women will wonder why the man has not bothered to ask. Again, it is more a difference in style rather than an indication of not caring.) But after a few hours of her attitude, it "gets to him" and he wants to leave. Finally, she blurts out some nasty remark which is the culmination of her unexpressed hurt from the other day. Now they decide they'd better talk. Let us assume this couple has already learned to communicate better than most. They sit down ready to hear each other's experiences, to learn how the other is feeling and why. As they go through where the problem began and the miscommunication that first took place, they are processing.

And now they have a chance of understanding and resolving their different interpretations of the same experience. Plus, they can work out a stop-gap strategy to make sure they don't *assume* what each other is thinking the next time, and in other future times.

In order to keep communication open, there is a skill which can be learned. It is the use of "I" statements. Many of us have learned that it is self-centered to talk about ourselves. But in order to have the other person receptive to what we are saying, it is necessary to talk about ourselves; if we make statements that are about the other person, they are likely to feel that they are being attacked. When someone feels attacked, it is only natural to defend oneself. This means that emotional energy gets stirred up to protect oneself from the attack - whether that attack is intentional or not. From a communication standpoint, what this amounts to is closing down and not being able to hear what is being said. The emotional reaction gets in the way of any rational thinking. By using "I" statements, this closing down, which takes place automatically without forethought, can be avoided.

An "I" statement is just that - it starts with "I" and continues to make reference to how the *speaker* is feeling or viewing a situation. Examples of this type of statement are:

- "I am upset with what's going on,"

- "I wish we had more time together," or

- "I find it so satisfying when you remember to call."

Notice that in the last example there is reference to "you." However, it is used in a descriptive fashion. It is okay to include the other person in an "I" statement, as long as it is descriptive and not judgmental or attacking. So, sentences like, "I think *you're* selfish" or "I think *you* could make more of an attempt to be helpful" do not fall under the umbrella of non-attacking statements. Many clients I have worked with, because they are so unaccustomed to speaking this way, often fall into the easy trap just cited. Let's look just a little bit further. The first sentence, "I think you're selfish" is clearly a put down. But what is wrong with the second one? Though it is subtle, it is still a put down because you are saying the other person is not helpful or has not made an attempt to be more helpful. But, it is a sentiment you feel and most likely believe is true. So how does that get expressed? A sentence more like, "I wish I could get a little more help" would be much more beneficial. Or, you could make a validation statement, which would be something like, "I'm sure you don't mean to upset me, but when you don't help with the dishes, I feel taken for granted."

Such a sentence is made up of three parts: the validation, the description, the feeling. The first part of the equation, the validation, is for the purposes of the other person not feeling attacked and consequently closing down. This part can either be very specific like, "I know you were very tired last night" or it can be generic as the one stated above (or something similar). The second portion is a description of the behavior on which you wish to comment. It is necessary that this portion be only descriptive in nature - no judgments. So, something like, "I know you don't mean to hurt me, but *your being so lazy*..." would not be helpful. In the last part, start with "I feel" and then say what you want.

Since they are your feelings, they can be whatever you want since you are "owning," taking responsibility, that these are your feelings. It is very important that this order be the one you use in your presentation. Presenting your point in any other sequence (like your feelings first) will again result in the person closing down and not hearing your point.

The following examples illustrate the best way to convey your issue to your partner:

A. "I know you've had a rough day, but when I don't get any help with the household chores I end up doing more than my share, and feel unappreciated."

B. "I know you don't mean to hurt me, but when you come home an hour late without calling, I get scared and can't attend to anything else that needs to get done."

At first, this style of talking will seem awkward. We have not been trained to speak this way. And to talk about ourselves may feel very difficult. For many of us, it is easier to point the finger at our partner rather than reveal our feelings. With practice, like everything else, this style of talking becomes easier to do. Additionally, communication will be smoother since defensiveness due to feeling attacked will be diminished. And perhaps most important of all, as we reveal our true feelings to our partner, a sense of intimacy is increased.

QUICK REFERENCE GUIDE TO COMMUNICATION TOOLS

- Communication is both expressive *and* receptive (sending and listening).

- Effective communication involves *active* listening: listening in a way that lets your partner know that you understand what (s)he is saying.

- Listening is most productive when it is done with openness and a respect for the other's point of view.

- No one is a mind reader; it is important to make a direct request.

- Do not assume that all your requests will be met simply because you have stated them clearly.

- Make requests in a respectful rather than demanding way.

- Be open (rather than making an assumption) about expectations, remembering that people are raised differently.

- Validate the other person's point of view - let them know you understand their perspective.

- Listen empathetically (with understanding) rather than trying to solve the problem.

- Use the skill of processing to clarify misunderstandings: listening and educating one another as to each person's experience.

- When a situation upsets you, use "I" statements and descriptions about the problem rather than attacking your partner.

- Express your feelings making sure to take responsibility for the fact that they are *your* feelings.

PART FOUR

WHEN ALL ELSE FAILS...

For some, you may have finished reading this book, tried some of the exercises, but still do not feel that your relationship has improved. Some of you may even feel that not much has changed. The first question you must ask of yourself is whether you have *truly* made the effort and *really* tried the ideas suggested in this book. It's not easy taking an honest look at oneself and perhaps finding that you did not do all that you could. That's okay. If you haven't really tried, there's no reason not to try again. This time, put forth a sincere effort and watch what happens.

Sadly, there will be others who can honestly say that they *have* made a sincere effort and yet have not reaped the benefits for which they had hoped. It may be that with all your attempts, your partner was still unresponsive. My experience tells me that if this is the case, it is probably because some issues from your partner's past are blocking them from being responsive. You would be best off talking to your partner (remembering to use "I" statements) about the efforts you have made and what you had hoped for. Ask your partner if these efforts were noticed. Perhaps, they weren't and you might, therefore, want to exaggerate them a bit more. Or, if they were noticed, perhaps they made your partner uneasy. If your partner indicates some sense of discomfort, get more information about how things could be done so as not to create this feeling. There may be ways that your partner would like to receive attention that were not included in this book. Talking about this will help you know what is more satisfying to your mate. It will also benefit your communication skills with one another. Even if no specifics come out of a conversation such as this, the fact that you are making an effort can still go a long way to helping to bring the two of you closer.

There may be situations where even all of your efforts do not help improve your relationship. If that is the case, it may be because your partner has some unresolved issues left over from childhood that are really standing in the way of any movement. With the awareness that this is not something that is being done intentionally by your partner, in a sensitive way, try to bring your partner's attention to the possibility of going for counseling. It is essential to remember that when raising such a possibility, you do so without making any judgments or saying things in such a way that will lead to your partner feeling bad. Such negative statements are likely to further block the idea of getting help.

Unfortunately, even with the kindest of approaches, some people are just too uncomfortable seeking professional help.

As much as it might benefit them, it will only do so if the person wants to make changes. Since you can only change yourself, you cannot effectively force your partner to get help. When you make a suggestion to your partner about getting help, be certain that you do not say anything indicating defectiveness (something wrong or faulty) about him or her. Here are some concrete examples of "wrong" and "right" ways to present the idea of professional help to your mate:

WRONG:

1. "I think there's really something wrong with you and you better go for help."

2. "I feel you have a problem."

3. "You have an issue that's getting in the way of us having a good relationship."

4. "Something from your childhood is still an issue, and I'm tired of it affecting our relationship."

(Notice that examples 1 and 2 seem like an "I" statement.

However, they are still clearly an attack on the other person; and therefore, will not be well received.)

RIGHT:

1. "We all have hurts from the past, which is certainly not a crime. But sometimes I think there may be some that still bother you and get in the way of our relationship. Would you consider talking to someone about them?"

2. "I have no doubt that you really want things to be better between us. Though I'm not sure, sometimes I think that the concern you have about _____ (your hurt feelings about your Dad, your fears of not having enough money, etc.) might be getting in the way. Maybe, talking to someone would help to look at things differently and clear them up for you."

3. "I want so much for things to be really good with us, but sometimes I wonder if we can do the work we need to do while the concerns you have about _____ (your feelings about your Mom, your fears of making changes, etc.) still bother you. I know lots of people are able to get past stuff when they talk to a professional. Would you think

about doing that?" Obviously, the specific words you choose will come across more sincerely, if they are your words. The suggestions given above under the "Right" category are just that - suggestions. But be aware that there are several concepts being used:

- Don't attack the other person or make them feel there is something wrong with them.

- Your language should be user-friendly rather than sounding like a "shrink."

- Offer suggestions or possible considerations rather than making a demand.

- Make the idea of going for help seem natural.

- Create a sense of hope for things between the two of you to be better; acknowledge your partner's desire for this goal also.

If this is the scenario you are facing, you might opt to leave things alone - temporarily. Sometimes, sensitive subjects are taken in slowly. A person being asked to face an issue that (s)he finds difficult, may need to do so in small doses. Of course, "temporarily" will mean different things to different people. Unfortunately, there is not a specific time guideline that can be offered. You will have to decide taking into consideration factors like how hard it is for you to keep living with things the way they are and how often you have raised the issue.

Further, I have worked with some people whose mates are just not able to face certain roadblocks. Certainly, this is a frustrating set of circumstances. As I have suggested to others, it is then time to do some self-exploration and reconsider *your* making personal adjustments to the relationship as it is. Though the latter idea may sound like support for choosing to live in misery, it is really one that is consistent with taking responsibility for your own life. Sure, some aspect of your mate might drive you crazy and you'd like to have it be different, but if adjusting to that trait is the only way to stay in the relationship, it might very well be the choice of preference. Additionally, accepting that this is a choice you've made goes a long way to not feeling trapped or helpless.

There is also the possibility that the two of you can go for counseling together. Many people will find this option more appealing than going on their own. It feels less like they are at fault or that they alone have a problem. Of course, it is quite possible that your partner would not be willing to try couple counseling either. Again, the idea of counseling may be too threatening; or, it may be because some people just don't believe in the benefits of counseling. But, unless there is a willingness to go, therapy rarely works, and if you cannot force someone into this situation they rarely cooperate with the therapist who's trying to help them. If this is the situation you find yourself in, you have the same options as were offered previously.

You do, of course, have the option of leaving the relationship. This is a drastic move and should be considered *only* when it becomes apparent that your mate is completely unwilling to change. Or, because the negative patterns are so ingrained, (s)he is unable to change. Making a decision to end a relationship is a subject that is beyond the scope of this book. It must be considered thoroughly from all facets and with ample consideration to all persons involved. The time, however, when ending the relationship should actually be elevated to a priority is if your predominant feeling is one of fear set off by the violent and/or abusive behavior of your mate. Abuse can be physical, sexual, verbal, or emotional. Unfortunately, relationships such as these probably will not respond to the skills offered in this book. However, if you are involved in such a toxic relationship, it is strongly advised that you seek counseling to explore what is best for you.

Fear can also take another form. That is, you may have seriously worked at your relationship and found that there really are differences or issues that cannot be resolved. You are quite certain that you are living in an empty marriage; that you and your spouse are more like longtime roommates than partners. Everything tells you that there is no hope for the marriage to be saved. Yet, you do nothing, out of the fear of starting over. It is hard to get divorced and it is hard to be alone. Everything you read says that divorce is bad for the children. Though the authors of this book are certainly advocates for keeping marriages together, there are instances when they must end. The most important thing is for you to consider all your options and their consequences rather than merely continuing to maintain behaviors out fear of change. Should you realize this is the case, it is strongly urged that you speak to a professional so that you can explore what is at the root of your fear and gain the strength to make a change - whether it be ending the marriage or staying in and trying to somehow salvage it.

Above all, please remember that you *do* have choices and you are never trapped, although you may feel this way. Just the fact that you have made the effort to read this book means you are willing to explore your choices and improve the quality of your life. This is an important first step and you should give yourself credit for what you have done so far.

Now it is time to think about and decide what your next steps will be.

SUMMARY REFERENCE GUIDE

- You need to put in a more committed effort at the suggestions provided in this book.

- The efforts you attempted were not really noted by your partner; adjustments can be made in your methods.

- Your partner has some unresolved issues that don't allow him or her to really be receptive; working with a professional may help.

- Consider going together for couple counseling.

- Explore more drastic measures after careful consideration if you determine that there is no possibility for working things out, especially if your relationship is toxic.

AFTERWORD

Marriage is indeed a wonderful thing. You've taken the most important first step towards ensuring a healthy marriage by reading this book. You've already made a great investment in your relationship. So now's the time to jump in and put this practical information to good use. Sometimes the best place to start is at the beginning. Go ahead and select an exercise you particularly liked and want to use with your mate.

Remember that if the exercise you select doesn't work right away, it's okay. You can try that same exercise again or you can always choose another one. This book is a tool you and your mate can rely on to provide the support your relationship needs. Don't forget that a good marriage needs attention and patience, and this is a great time to get started. You can do it!

ABOUT THE AUTHORS

Karen Sherman, Ph.D. is a licensed psychologist in New York, specializing in relationships since 1982. Her approach has always been skills-based and focused on helping couples understand their stylistic differences. Through her website, **www.ChoiceRelationships.com**, Karen offers several free tools to help couples as well as other products to enhance their relationship.

Karen is a sought after expert in the media and offers her knowledge in blogs at ThirdAge.com, a column and podcasts on Hitchedmag.com, and articles on ClubMom.com.

Aside from relationships, Karen also does work with individuals helping them get past their past to live a life of choice. A second area of interest is in the area of stress reduction since that has such an impact on one's life and relationship. She is a contributing author to *101 Great Ways to Improve Your Life, Vol. 2.*

She provides consultations both in-person and on the phone, teleseminars, and workshops. Learn more at **www.drkarensherman. com**

Trained as a Speech/Language Pathologist, **Dale Klein** has worked in both clinical and managerial capacities for nearly two decades. Today, she is a sought-after speaker/consultant on a local and national level, and has served as an Adjunct Professor at two local colleges.

Dale is the founder and owner of **Profitable Speech, LLC** which she established in 1994. As a Corporate Communication & Speech Specialist, she works with individuals as well as groups and conducts high-energy, information-packed workshops and webinars. She focuses on furthering the success of her clients in the following areas:

- Public speaking

- Presentation pointers

- Networking skills

- Voice coaching

- Interviewing techniques

- Interpersonal dynamics

- Meeting facilitation

- Foreign accent reduction

When people want to stand out from the competition, they call Dale Klein.

Learn more about what Dale can offer you by visiting her online at: www.profitablespeech.com and be sure to tune in to her ongoing podcasts.

BIBLIOGRAPHY

Gottman, J.M. and Silver, N. <u>The Seven Principles for Making Marriage Work,</u> 2000. Three Rivers Press, New York City.

Gray, J. <u>Men are From Mars, Women are From Venus</u>, 1992, HarperCollins Publishers, New York

Kelleher, K. "Dissecting the Dysfunctions That Lead Down the Path to Divorce," LA Times, September 18, 2000

Love, P. and Stosny, S. <u>How to Improve Your Marriage Without Talking About It</u>, 2007. Broadway Books, New York

Roberts, L.J. "Fire and Ice Both Detrimental in Marital Communication," Journal of Marriage and Family, August 2000

Tanner, L. "Men Listen With Half of Brain," 86th Scientific Assembly & Annual Meeting of the Radiological Society of North America, November 28, 2000

Waite, L.J. and Gallagher, M. <u>The Case for Marriage: Why Married People are Happier, Healthier, and Better Off Financially,</u> 2001, Broadway Books, New York City

FREE BONUS GIFTS

Four FREE Bonuses Included With Your Purchase!

To help you enhance your relationship further, Dr. Karen at www.ChoiceRelationships.com or www.drkarensherman.com is offering you …

Bonus # 1:

Nine Tips Guaranteed to Bring Back the Fun, Joy, and Connection You Had in Your Relationship When You First Fell in Love (PDF file)

Bonus # 2:

Taking Care of Business… How to Create a Great Relationship With Easy to Use Tools as presented live on WCWP FM radio (MP3 download)

To claim bonuses 1 and 2 go to this link:

http://choicerelationships.com/marriagemagic/drkaren/

One of the best ways to improve your relationships is by strengthening your listening skills. When you receive your 2 free bonuses from Dale Klein, M.A., Corporate Communication & Speech Specialist, here's what you can look forward to:

Bonus # 3:

Listening Essentials—a clear and informative guide that reveals:

- Benefits of listening

- Barriers to listening

- Techniques to improve your listening

Bonus # 4:

Listen Up: Leveraging Your Listening Skills is More than Hearsay--an audio file (MP3) that uncovers why listening is so challenging in our day-to-day lives and the impact of not listening well.

To claim Bonuses 3 and 4, go to this link:

http://choicerelationships.com/marriagemagic/dale/

INDEX

CPSIA information can be obtained at www.ICGtesting.com
Printed in the USA
BVOW021135071212

307478BV00001B/6/A